Let's find why

A practical guide to action-research in schools

Christine Macintyre

Moray House Publications
Holyrood Road, Edinburgh
EH8 8AQ

Moray House
Publications

A full list of titles is available from

The Publications Officer
Moray House Publications
Holyrood Road
Edinburgh EH8 8AQ
tel: 0131-558 6398
fax: 0131-558 3428

Some new titles for publication during 1995

Specific Learning Difficulties (Dyslexia)
by Gavin Reid
Volume 1: Assessment, Teaching and the Curriculum
Volume 2: Literacy, Language and Learning
Spotlights on Practice - (90 minute video)

Gender and Special Educational Needs
by Gwynedd Lloyd

Practical Phonology
by Dorothea Bogle

Tactile Graphics
by Ron Hinton

Group Textual Study of Fiction Series:
Carrie's War
by Nina Bawden
So Far From Skye
by Judith O'Neill

Primex Version 2.5
by Tom Conlon

Acknowledgements

My thanks go to all the teachers and student teachers who discussed their ideas and generously shared their research findings. I have tried to record these accurately. I hope I have.

Thank you too, to Dr. Sylvia Jackson, Mrs Helen Fraser and Dr. Donald Bligh, colleagues who provided constructive criticism and support during the preparatory stages of the text.

And finally thank you to the staff of the Publications Unit at Moray House for their patience and for the professional presentation of the manuscript.

C.M.

First published 1991
Reprinted 1995
Reprinted 1998
ISBN 0 9015 80 35X
© Christine Macintyre 1991

Printed and bound by Bell and Bain Ltd, Glasgow

Contents

Preface

This text is primarily for teachers and student teachers. It aims to help those who are immersed in their own classrooms carry out a small scale piece of action-research so that they may understand and improve an aspect of their practice and through that the learning experiences of their pupils. In this mode, teachers get to grips with choosing a research 'problem' by reflecting on their own practice and evaluating it in the light of their professional expertise and in the full understanding of their pupils' needs. The action that follows is grounded in theoretical knowledge so that it is likely to improve the status quo. Evidence on whether or not the anticipated improvement has occurred is gathered in the evaluation phase.

The process itself is similar to that adopted by reflective teachers who seek to improve or extend their performance. The difference comes in the careful application of the principles of action-research. This ensures that teachers may move beyond giving descriptions of what occurred in their classrooms to providing explanations. They can, with confidence, say they have found why........

Action-research then, is one logical outcome of self-appraisal as the examples in the text show. The text relies heavily on the experiences of busy classroom teachers and student-teachers trying action-research for the first time. It is a basic text written to encourage teachers to become teacher/researchers. I hope it does.

Christine Macintyre

1

Four teachers tell......

Teachers have the responsibility for providing the best possible education for quite a large number of children who differ in their attitude and motivation to learning as well as in their capacity to learn. No-one would deny that this is a highly complex and demanding task. In addition they are expected to respond positively to new teaching initiatives and to master new skills so that their pupils may benefit from new thinking and new teaching practices. Staff development and self-appraisal are further demands. *Can teachers really be expected to be researchers as well?*

Before the answer 'No' resounds, it might be useful to try to answer the question, *"What can teachers gain from carrying out research in their classrooms?"* and see whether the advantages outweigh the disadvantages (i.e. time taken in thinking, reading and planning), if disadvantages they be. Below are extracts from the reactions of four teachers who have been asked to carry out a piece of action-research as part of a pilot study which was designed to monitor teachers' evaluations and concerns as they adopted the dual teacher/researcher role. The four are reporting back to each other in an informal setting.

Firstly Jean, an experienced learning support teacher who selected Kevin, aged 12, as her 'subject' and motor impairment as her research topic. Jean explained,

"I knew Kevin was clumsy . . . he drove us all mad falling over his feet and bumping into things. His books were a terrible mess and he didn't seem to care that they were torn and dirty. He said he didn't like sports and it was difficult to find anything positive to talk about. He did ride his bike to school but he never looked confident or particularly safe. For my research I made Kevin the subject of my Case Study and I observed him closely, hopefully unobtrusively, in as many different situations as I could. I wanted to build up a picture of how Kevin coped during the day. Maybe knowing

1

he was having problems at school made his clumsiness worse, maybe he was just growing fast but I had a suspicion that this was more than adolescence. . . his behaviour in class was deteriorating too.

At first the playground observations didn't reveal much because he just seemed to hang around for most of the time. However, during an icy spell it was obvious that Kevin had great difficulty keeping his feet; he was very tentative and unsure. Then later, on a fine day, he tried to jump onto the school bus and missed his footing completely. It could have been a nasty accident. That's when I decided that observation should stop and finding out should begin.

The PE teacher and I did some tests of motor impairment, the Henderson revision of the Stott Tests, to see if we could find what was wrong. We had suspected poor co-ordination but we weren't sure. My early research question was 'Why is Kevin clumsy?' and later I refined this to 'Will activities specifically designed to help balance, help Kevin?' In the event, as this question was being thought about, the Stott tests showed that Kevin had a very poor sense of balance and building on examples given in the book we produced an activity programme specially to develop balance. We arranged for Kevin and a small group of others to take part for 15 minutes every day at lunchtime. Some of the other teachers took a turn to help with the group. I monitored his progress over six weeks. During that time, I also noticed he was inclined to rush at tasks and so I encouraged him to slow down and try to plan what he was going to do.

It was difficult to know whether it was the balance activities or the slowing down or the extra attention which helped Kevin - maybe it was all three. The main thing was that Kevin appeared to be less awkward and frustrated. His other teachers said things were better and he seemed happier and more confident."

As a learning support teacher Jean had probably more opportunities than a class teacher for sustained one-to-one interaction. She was glad that she had taken the opportunity to find out about motor impairment because she suspected that early diagnosis and remediation could help youngsters like Kevin to cope more easily. The research had been time-consuming but other teachers helping out for one activity session per week had made it possible. They had become interested in the programme too. Jean had gained a much deeper understanding about motor impairment and became more confident in being able to take steps to diagnose problems in this field. She was also surprised and delighted to find that other teachers were very interested in the 'clumsy child' syndrome and anxious to find out about remediation. And so an individual interest and action became a collaborative venture, and as a result several teachers and children benefited from the research.

The second teacher was Bill, a very experienced teacher of French, mainly to Yr 1 & Yr 2 classes. He told his research story...

"My head of department had suggested on several occasions that I should organise my class into groups and have a change from teaching the whole class. He meant mixed-ability groups, and I just had a gut feeling that wouldn't work so I overlooked the suggestion.......by mistake! However, when I said I'd try out a bit of research and I needed a research topic, I thought I'd give group work a go. Well I reorganised 2b and it was grim. Kids in one group flatly refused to sit beside one another. In another group they sat alright but they just worked individually. And I was run off my feet repeating instructions and trying to keep the noise down .. doing all the things I knew would happen. I nearly gave up, but being in this group (the pilot research group) and knowing I had to come and report back, I thought I'd better persevere!

Well it got a bit better. Once they knew what was expected of them things began to improve. I also designed things like researching a topic from a number of books, building group word banks, and listening at the listening centre. Infact my research question became 'What activities can encourage second years to collaborate in developing their understanding in French?' Their vocabulary was too limited to do much in the way of conversations, but the groups did gel after a bit. The best 'unforeseen advantage'

*was finding one bright lad actually re-teaching one of the
slower ones. He (i.e. the slower one) didn't seem to resent
this, in fact he may have preferred that to my looking over
his shoulder..'*

*One of the things these groups are supposed to develop
is group interaction and communication. Well, that certainly
happened, ...although not too much of it was in French!"*

Although Bill reverted to whole class teaching for much of the
time after his research, he said that gathering evidence and giving
the idea a genuine try to find whether it worked, had helped him to
show that his own preferred organisation was best for him. Being
able to report a trialling process rather than just avoiding this issue
was a bonus. Bill was awaiting developments. He anticipated that
despite his research, ' introducing group work' might still feature
in his appraisal, but hoped not! (The issue of whether those in
authority would pay attention to research findings concerned all
the researchers!)

Thirdly Kate, a first year probationer of P5 who was perplexed
and anxious. She explained,

*"My class was dull. The children all did what they were
told, there were no discipline problems, but there was no
animation either. And so after a great deal of thought and
reflection I decided that the way to improve the pupils' oral
contribution was to concentrate on my own questioning. I
realised from listening to tape recordings of my lessons that
when asked questions, the pupils tended to produce only
'Yes' or 'No' answers. I needed to encourage the pupils to
tell me what they were thinking. In that way I could find
what was important to them. I thought that better questions
would help this process.*

*And so for my research I prepared a number of higher-
order questions which I thought would do the trick and
during my project work I settled down with one group and
had the tape-recorder ready to record the pupils' longer
and more thoughtful replies. They didn't happen. Eventually I told the pupils what I had done and asked them what*

4

was wrong and was surprised to find that they only liked 'easy questions'. When they knew 'difficult questions' were on line they "clammed up", their minds "went blank" and they preferred not to answer. They told me that they hated speaking out in case they were wrong and so I had to find other strategies. I am at the minute trying to set up discussions where the pupils choose the topics. Hopefully this will encourage them to say more. I used Dillon's work mainly to develop this idea."

Kate's research had arisen from her reflecting on her own professional competence in the classroom, taking steps to get things better and evaluating the outcome. As her first idea was unsuccessful, she had amended her research question from 'Do higher-order questions produce better responses' to 'What strategies can I try to encourage the pupils to respond?' She considered that this kind of experience would help her do three things. Firstly it would help her to understand the children's interaction and so enable her to make it more enjoyable and fruitful. Secondly, reflecting on her own practice would develop her self-appraisal skills. Thirdly she vowed that having identified a problem and having tried ways of investigating the cause, she would not rest until she had overcome it!

And lastly Rob, a Guidance Teacher for Yr 4 gave this account.

"Recently a lot of publicity has been given to stress in teaching and this made me wonder what aspects of school life our pupils found stressful and how they coped. I realised that this could be quite a sensitive area and I anticipated that the pupils might be inhibited on two counts - one, a natural reluctance to admit failing to cope when others were obviously doing so, and two, a fear that saying the school was allowing stress to go unchecked could be interpreted as a criticism of the Guidance Staff in particular. And so I designed a questionnaire and gave it to all the pupils in the fourth year. I distributed it in class so that they would take time and have privacy to complete it. The privacy angle was

important as well as getting the questionnaires back from everyone.

To try to help them answer honestly I explained beforehand that everyone had something that caused them anxiety - I certainly had! I also pointed out that while the questionnaire was only about stress in school, they could discuss anything that was worrying them with specially trained counsellors. Also I explained that the school's duty was to try to make school a good place to be and the results would be used to improve whatever was causing difficulty. The pupils knew the results were confidential but if anyone wanted to talk with me they could put their name on the sheet and I would arrange that.

In an area of high unemployment I had expected that most of the anxieties would concern getting qualifications for jobs and this was so. But leaving home and not getting enough money to get decent digs was important too. They wanted interesting jobs, jobs working with people rather than routine jobs like "bank, insurance, factory work and supermarkets". Interestingly, several pupils reported being "fed up because of 'slack' teachers" and to the question "What do you do when this happens?", they replied, "Bunk off", "fool around", or "I don't do any work!" The coping strategies the pupils used often exacerbated the very situation they resented. What I did was to make these kinds of issues the subject of discussion in the P.S.D. (Personal and Social Development) programme. I think the pupils were more interested because they knew that the topics concerned their own welfare.

Despite the exam pressure in Yr 4, the pupils in these discussions considered Yrs 1 and 2 were much more stressful because "you didn't know if you were going to make the grade and too many things were new." Also "you never knew if your friend was going to go off with someone else." By Yr 4 they had come to terms with hopes and aspirations, they didn't think that school itself was too stressful or they were prepared to accept the stress as unavoidable, for as one pupil explained in a resigned tone, "It's all hassle from now on. . ."

Rob evaluated his time as researcher positively and claimed that the pupils appreciated having their accounts treated respectfully. The results making 'a good PSD programme' was a definite bonus. He had shared the results with the staff and hoped that they had provided cause for thought and action. The main difficulty had been formulating questions for the questionnaire. He did this in the evening so that the research didn't take up too much teaching time. In retrospect Rob found that this was balanced out by the pupils' replies providing the focus for discussion. This saved preparation time. He wondered whether a bank of questions or even of sample questionnaires could be made. Rob particularly valued getting feedback from the pupils. He made it known that the pupils' concerns had been noted and acted upon and he intended to write a questionnaire for Yr 2 on the advice of Yr 4 i.e. because in Yr 4's estimation, that was the time of greatest stress.

The four teachers all spoke of the hard work in conceptualising their research and carrying it through but they did feel that they had benefited from acquiring a new skill, from having the responsibility of starting something off and seeing it through, from having the opportunity to be creative, from having greater confidence in explaining why top-down suggestions did not work for everyone and generally in having a deeper understanding of the aspect of teaching or learning which they had studied. Above all they valued having improved the learning experiences of their pupils.

These four thumbnail sketches also show that research in the classroom can involve one child or one group, a whole class or a year group. It can mean the researcher observing one child for a long period of time or data can be collected on one occasion only. Teachers can choose any aspect of classroom or professional life that they please and design ways both to investigate the issue and to take action to understand and hopefully to improve the situation.

Action- research in classrooms then can be:

- *Creative*
- *Realistic*
- *Rigorous*

- *Contextualised*
- *Flexible*
- *Illuminating*

- *Creative* ... because teachers themselves can choose a topic which is intriguing and challenging as well as being appropriate for the pupils involved! They can take time to shape ideas and action-plans until the 'best' way forward i.e. the way to make things better, crystalises. Many teachers find this creative potential stimulating and refreshing. They enjoy 'finding why' in their own way.

- *Contextualised* ... because the whole plan is thought through by teachers in their own classrooms i.e. people who know the day to day planning, the pupils who are to be involved and the classroom organisation which exists. Therefore the action can be totally meaningful ... it may even be absorbed into the daily routine so that it is a natural part of teaching, with of course the added care in monitoring and recording the course of events.

- *Realistic* ... because the intimate knowledge of the context allows teachers to gauge what *needs* to be done and what *can* be done 'midst all the other pressures of the day. A small-scale study which really tackles an issue is best for beginners. Using a sledge hammer to crack a nut is definitely not part of an action-research plan!

- *Flexible* ... because it can adapt to unforeseen circumstances. Very often the action in action-research is planned to happen at a certain time each week, but if other contingencies arise then it is likely that the research can be moved to another spot. This would depend of course whether the time of day was important to the research findings, whether other, perhaps specialist teachers were involved as co-researchers or whether cover was needed if the children participating in the research had to come out of the classroom. These considerations aside, a measure of flexibility is generally possible and this can be important in getting the research completed without unnecessary stress.

- *Rigorous* ... because if the results of the research are to be credible and stand scrutiny, then all the stages i.e. the planning, the implementation and the evaluation must be carried out according to the principles implicit in the term 'action-research'. *These principles (i.e. that the research must contain an action to improve the situation, that the action should be informed by reading and that concern to reduce bias in the collection of data should be inbuilt)* are explained in the chapters that follow.

- *Illuminating* ... because if these principles *are* adhered to, action-researches can go beyond the level of *description* and begin to *explain* why things are as they are. Just unlocking one key or discovering one nugget (rather than a gold mine) can be tremendously revealing and exciting and make all the hard work worthwhile.

To allow this action-research to happen then, a basic understanding of what is involved is essential and this text sets out to provide this starter knowledge. Whenever possible, examples from recent research in classrooms are used to encourage hesitant or doubting or new researchers to try!

2

What is action-research?

Action-research is an *investigation* where, as a result of rigorous self-appraisal and analysis of current practice, the researcher *focuses* on a *'problem'* (or a topic or an issue which needs to be explained) and on the basis of *information* (about the up-to-date state of the art, about the people who will be involved and about the context), *plans, implements and evaluates* an *action*, then *draws conclusions* on the basis of the findings.

This is not a linear process however, for action-research has the capacity to respond to factors which emerge during the planning and implementation of the research. Figure 1 shows this gradual process of decision-making. It attempts to portray the flexibility which allows the researcher to respond both to the context and to the responses of those being studied.

Fig1: An action-research cycle

Reflection and analysis of current practice.

General idea of research topic and context.

Narrowing down the topic, planning the action.

Scanning the literature, discussing with colleagues

Refined topic - selection of key texts, formulation of research question/ hypothesis, organisation of refined action-plan in context.

Tentative action-plan, consideration of different research strategies.

Take action.
Monitor effects - evaluation of strategy and research question/hypothesis.
Final amendment.

Final action

Evaluation of entire process.

Conclusions, claims, explanations.

Recommendations for further research.

The first part of the diagram describes the planning process and involves the researcher in;

- reflecting on current teaching and as a result of self-appraisal/ analysis, choosing a research topic i.e. one which focuses on an aspect of school or classroom life, and considering it in context. Later this topic may be narrowed down to make it manageable (e.g. by involving only one group of children or one curriculum area in the investigation);

- formulating and constantly reconsidering a research question/ hypothesis in the light of the advice given in the literature and in the knowledge of the chosen subjects and the context;

- planning and taking an action and possibly modifying it follow- ing evaluation of its effects;

- choosing the most appropriate data gathering instruments and planning how bias can best be reduced in the collection of data.

This model supposes that teachers are the researchers in their own classrooms. Then they already understand the children and the learning and social contexts. This enables then to make realistic judgements about the parameters of the research e.g. the scale of the action, the numbers to be involved, the time span, the most appropriate data gathering strategies. Teachers new to teach- ing generally or in a new context will probably need more time to observe and evaluate before they can begin to identify a research problem. Thereafter the procedure will be the same.

▼▼▼Choosing a topic

The first important decision in confronting a piece of action- research is to decide on the topic. As there are many possibilities it may help you to consider different categories and select an idea from one depending on whether you wish

- *to identify and improve one teaching competency* e.g. planning, organising, discussing, questioning, motivating, responding, pacing, time-management etc.....or

- *to extend one aspect of your teaching in a particular way* e.g. by introducing self-assessment for one group of pupils in one curriculum area; by attempting to raise the self-esteem of pupils who lack confidence in their ability to learn; by examining the learning involved in problem- solving and devising appropriate 'problems' for certain children; by incorporating a movement skills component into classroom work for a clumsy child etc......or

- *to contribute to or to evaluate policy making* e.g. by finding out what parents who are invited to participate in school life want to do; to monitor the effects of teaching/learning where adults and pupils learn together; to evaluate the realism of teachers and social workers working together to provide a better environment for children; to gather parents' perceptions of being involved in School Boards etc.

The choice of topic is very important. It should be stimulating and challenging yet at the same time provide an 'action' which is realistic and manageable. The research topic has to be identified and refined, a research question(s) or hypothesis has to be formulated so that the investigation has a clear focus, research procedures have to be planned and data or evidence has to be gathered and analysed. The decision is yours - one type of investigation is not 'better' or easier than another, it is simply advisable to consider the scale of the undertaking in advance and to weigh the advantages and disadvantages of one against the other. This should help you to make an informed choice.

▼▼▼Formulating a research question

The topic chosen, the next step is to consider the research question. One strategy which seems to help researchers to decide on their research question(s) is for them to ask *WHY?* i.e. 'Why have I chosen this topic for my research?' and then to define the answer in terms of the subjects' improved experience. This also helps to indicate the research action which could be taken.

Alongside the common-sense or 'derived from experience' answer to the question Why?, the literature can help in justifying the choice by showing that the proposed investigation is suitable for the subjects in their context and in the time scale available. This process is now shown in diagrammatic form. Note how the two 'sides' of the process, i.e. reading the literature and formulating a research question mirror each other, beginning wide and narrowing in focus as the research question is refined.

Fig 2: Formulating a research-question

General notion of topic

Scanning the literature.

Selecting key texts.

Reading to justify, to explain and to guide the action plan.

Reading to compare findings.

What do I wish to find out ?

Ask **why?** and answer in terms of the subjects' new and improved experiences and so clarify the purpose of the research.

Consider the research idea in context.

Plan what action should be taken to improve the situation and to provide evidence to answer the research question.

Research question

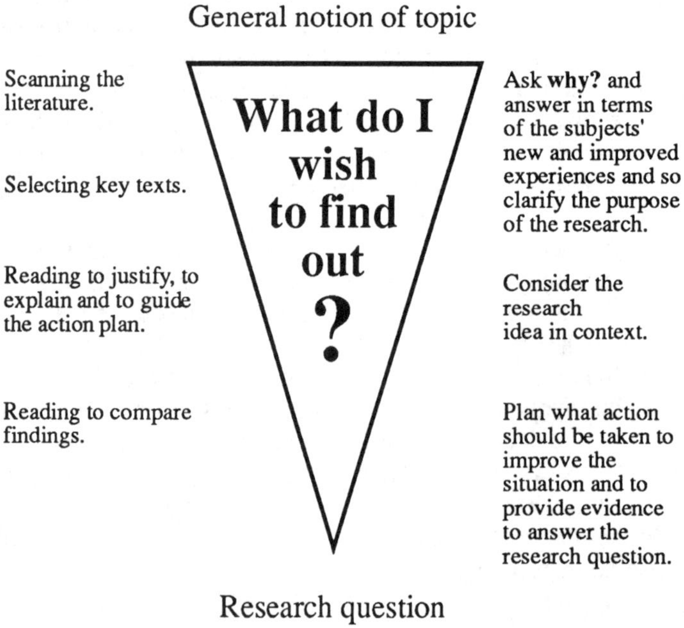

Some brief examples from transcriptions from interviews with teachers trying to formulate research questions for the first time now follow to help clarify the procedure. Texts which were used to guide each piece of action-research are given in the bibliography.

Example 1 - Creative Writing R = *Researcher* I = *Interviewer*

R   I'd like to try self-assessment.
I   Why?
R   Because I'd like to understand more about the diagnostic possibilities of self-assessment. Thinking back I feel that teachers spend a lot of time assessing and the children don't read what they write so it's a waste of time.
I   Why is that?
R   For one thing, that piece of writing or whatever is finished now and they are on to something else . . . or maybe the teacher has just written 'good' because in creative writing it's difficult to know what to say.....
I   What would you see as the benefit of self-assessment? (i.e. clarifying the *purpose* of the research).
R   Well, the pupils would be able to explain what was important to them in their story, while they were writing or immediately after . . . The teachers would find out what criteria the pupils were using to assess their own work and whether they were the same as their own.

Research questions

Stage 1
*   What criteria do these children use to assess their own work?... (i.e. in creative writing)
*   What criteria do I use to assess creative writing?
*   What shall I do if they are different?

Stage 2 (These questions are the refined editions of stage 1, i.e. after they have been considered in context. In this case they indicate the number of children and implicitly the scale of the investigation).
*   What criteria do these three children use to assess their own pieces of creative writing?
*   Is there a match or mismatch with my own choice?

Action:
Discussions with the children a) to identify *their* criteria and b) to resolve or acknowledge any discrepancies so that teacher and children are working together to achieve the same goals.

Example 2: Study Skills

R   I'd like to look at study skills.
I   Why?
R   Well these pupils are coming up to exams. They also have some assignments to do at home so it would help them to organise their work better . . .(pause) but it's not really organisation I'm after. At the moment we tell them to set aside time and to try to have a clear space to work but I'm thinking of more helpful techniques. Some of the pupils develop these for themselves - I'm sure they could be taught - if I knew what they were.
I   So you are really asking "What techniques do pupils need to develop to help them be more efficient learners?"
R   I have some ideas, like reading the question carefully and underlining the key words and making sure they are covered in the answer . . . and I'm sure there are others like this which would be helpful.
I   Do you think the pupils have already developed strategies which they would be keen to share?
R   Well, if I knew what these were, I could look for others. There's quite a lot written about study skills, isn't there?

Research questions
Stage 1
*   What techniques can help pupils to be more efficient learners?
*   Do the pupils already use a number of these - what are they?
*   Can they usefully be shared?

Action and Evaluation:
The pupils complete assignments using the different techniques identified above e.g. reading the question several times, underlining key words and discussing them all. *Evaluation* - Using this technique, have the assignments improved? Do the pupils consider that this has helped them to structure their work?

Stage 2
*   What techniques do the pupils consider most helpful in planning their learning?

Example 3: Play in the Nursery School

R I'd like to look at children's play in the Nursery School.
I Why does that interest you?
R Well it's not easy to decide when to intervene in children's play and if you do, to know how to extend the children's learning. I'm not convinced that teachers should intervene at all, maybe the children should be left alone. But as a teacher I almost feel pressurised to do *something*....certainly if other adults are in the room........ it's expected.......
I So you would want to justify intervening or not in children's play - and you would need to know what you meant by intervention.
R Yes . . . and then carrying the learning on afterwards . . .

Research questions
Stage 1
• In what ways can teacher intervention extend or inhibit children's learning during play?

Action :
The teacher selected two very different ways of intervening from a considered range of possibilities.These were

a. Providing appropriate resources but not taking part e.g.-adding a toy to the sand when the child's interest was beginning to wane, then withdrawing to an observation post.
and
b. Taking a role when 'instructed' by the pupils e.g. joining in imaginative play in the House Corner.

Stage 2
• Can, and in what ways can providing appropriate resources (i.e. in line with the child's activity) extend the child's learning?
• Can role-playing help the teacher to extend the children's learning during Nursery play?

Action:
Observation, recording and evaluation of the quality of the responses to the different kinds of interventions which were made.

Example 3 - Social integration of three children from the Punjab

T   I have three Punjabi children newly arrived in my P3 class. They understand English but don't talk much... naturally they stay together and then they speak in their own language. One child is very withdrawn. I'd like to help them to mix with the other children and for them to feel we value their culture.

I   So you want to find what strategies would help their social integration and you would like to know what others have tried?

T   That will help because it's difficult to know what to do with such young children with poor spoken English ...... they can't really *explain* aspects of their culture to the other children... so I'm at a loss for ideas.

I   Have you asked the children themselves or spoken with the parents to see what they would prefer you to do?

T   I think I'll do that first in case I inadvertently offend anyone.

Research question
Stage 1
• What do the children and their parents consider would be the best way to help the social integration of these three children?

Action:
Informal discussion with the children and parents to gather information on ways forward.

and
• How can the teacher convey that the classroom will be genuinely enriched by knowing more about the children's culture?

Action:
Carrying out the ideas (suggested by the children and their parents and checked in the literature) and observing the children carefully to note their reactions during the interactions and during subsequent social times in the class and in the playground to see if social interaction improves.

(The parents came into school to tell the children about a Punjabi wedding and this broke some ice. But in effect the most

18

successful breakthrough for the withdrawn child came when the teacher learned to count from 1 - 10 in Punjabi. The child was delighted that the teacher had taken the trouble to do this... he helped her with pronunciation and later was persuaded to teach an English speaking child one or two numbers. The teacher considered that the child's confidence had been boosted as a result and a better relationship was formed from that time).

Formulating an interesting and potentially useful research question is certainly a critical part of the research process because the research action is planned to provide evidence or data to answer that question. No other information, no matter how interesting or diverting, contributes to the research. The findings must answer the research question. If it is amended in context in response to what has been discovered then that is a positive step, but the researchers must make a conscious decision about the change not just drift into something new. The penalty for doing that is discovering that the data is useless because it does not answer the research question.

Remember Kate? She altered her research question from "Do higher-order questions produce better responses from the pupils?" to "What strategies can I try to encourage the pupils to respond?" This widening out was in response to her findings that higher-order questions were not producing the anticipated improvement in pupil performance. She had planned and considered the implications of the change and she recorded it carefully in her research report.

Deciding on a research question *is* difficult. Do not be surprised if it takes some time. Take comfort from Dillon (1985) who says

"By the time of advanced graduate study, students have answered thousands upon thousands of questions, only to have a time of it thinking up a single question to ask for their thesis"

Let's find why

▼▼▼Formulating a hypothesis

An alternative model to the research question is one based on the formulation of a hypothesis i.e. a testable idea.   Usually a relationship between two variables is postulated (e.g. If I do X then Y results) and then tested by gathering evidence. The hypothesis testing procedure is often selected if the researcher has a realistic notion of what the outcome of the investigation could be or if one procedure only is to be investigated.

In this mode the researcher may wish to test someone else's research findings in their own context. The new investigation may then add to or detract from the credibility of the original research or extend the knowledge base. It is a model which, in stipulating the outcome in advance, denies any alteration or amendment during the process of the research.   The hypothesis is either confirmed or denied and the evidence to support or negate the claim is clearly documented. As with the research question model, the hypothesis emerges from reading the literature, reflecting on experience and from discussion with people knowledgeable in the field.

Examples
1. 'That the use of higher-order questions will stimulate the pupils to give resourceful responses.'

In this investigation, the researcher would carefully monitor the pupils' responses to prepared higher-order questions. This would test the hypothesis,

"If I ask higher order questions (about_____ in_____)the pupils will be stimulated to respond   e.g. by drawing on incidents in their own experience and sharing these with their peers."

Action:
Preparation of higher-order questions. Organisation and recording of teacher/pupil interaction. Evaluation.

If longer and more thoughtful responses occurred, then the hypothesis was confirmed (i.e.for these pupils in that particular

20

situation). If no improvement took place then the hypothesis was denied. Once the result was known and the reasons investigated, the researcher would not go on to try out other ways of stimulating responses....only the research question would have this kind of flexibility.

2. a 'That pupils in P4 will be able to articulate the criteria they use to assess their creative writing.'

   b 'That there will be a match between the pupils' and the teacher's choice.'

3. That 'social worries' will outweigh 'academic worries' in the pupils anticipating transition to secondary school.

If, as in Example 3, the variables could be open to misinterpretation, they should be carefully explained. This procedure is called 'operationalising the hypothesis.'

e.g. academic worries 1. new subjects
                        2. not coping
                        3. poor marks

      social worries   1. bullying
                        2. failure to make friends
                        3. getting lost

In some ways the two strategies are similar i.e. they both require the researchers to narrow down their field until particular variables or questions have been identified. They differ however in the timing of the final version - the research question model having the capacity to react to the pupils' unexpected responses or to the teachers shifting the focus or locus of their investigation. The reaction involves amending the question to take account of developments as they occur.

▼▼▼Reviewing the literature

Experienced teachers, through reflection and analysis of their classroom practices may be able, quite readily, to decide on a research topic and plan an appropriate remedial action to enrich the learning environment for their pupils. Even then, they will benefit from studying the literature associated with the topic because this can show what other researchers have found, what strategies have been successful and what pitfalls should be avoided.

Researchers reporting in journals often share their research questions, their data gathering strategies and their findings. This means that others can benefit from their experiences. Additionally they may offer an evaluation of their own process and in the light of this make recommendations for further research. This guidance could be immensely useful to a subsequent study, saving unnecessary and unprofitable repetition and possibly providing other ideas than those first considered. If potential researchers can be aware of up-to-date findings in this way, then their research plans can take knowledge forward rather than lead them to rediscovering the wheel.

Alternatively, ideas for research topics can be suggested by the literature itself i.e. by articles in journals, in books, in policy documents and in research reports. Such readings can implicitly suggest possible research actions.

It can be understood, then, why one of the principles of action - research is that the process is informed by the literature. This helps to ensure that the planning process has substance. It prevents researchers just plucking an idea from the sky and having a go, and then being disappointed by the results. Research can, of course, be planned to duplicate aspects of previous studies (e.g. finding out if and how results claimed from one investigation vary in another situation - say in monitoring the behaviour of privileged and underprivileged children), but there is in this kind of situation still an element of surprise, something new to be discovered and added to the original knowledge base. The literature can still help in the adaptation of the original plan to suit the new context.

The literature then can

- *Show what has already been done in the particular area.*

- *Provide an idea for a research topic, or show that the one chosen by reflecting on current events in the classroom or self-appraisal is sound.*

- *Justify the suitability of the topic for the particular subjects.*

- *Provide starter points for new research.*

- *Provide ideas for planning the action.*

- *Give the researcher confidence that the topic is worth investigating and that the potential for discovering something or for planning something or evaluating something worthwhile is there.*

It can be a particularly daunting experience to have a research idea (or to be setting out to the library to find a research idea) and to enter the library to be faced with shelves of books all seemingly bursting with critical thinking and good, if sometimes conflicting, advice. Even worse, to find there is no information on your specific idea at all! In this case it is best to carefully reconsider the idea and see whether you have indeed identified an original focus for your investigation, or, and sadly this is more likely, whether the idea is suspect.

Given that there *is* enough recent literature to give you guidance and set you thinking, it can be helpful to think of the literature review as a process which mirrors the general research idea becoming refined into a specific research topic and question/ hypotheses i.e. one which moves from wide to narrow.

Stage 1: Scanning the field
The first stage involves scanning the different kinds of literature to find information about the topic, to find e.g. what recent developments there have been and what they claim to have achieved; what kinds of research studies have taken place; what research strategies were used and where they occurred. The British Educational Index is a particularly rich and helpful source of information indicating

where specific readings may be found. All of this information helps a researcher plan an appropriate new investigation.

Librarians are often very interested in research and from their wide knowledge of texts can suggest where relevant readings may be found. If computer facilities are available and if you can provide key words to pinpoint your area of investigation, then a computer search for sources of information is possible. Texts may also be available on inter-library loan. The subject index in a text often provides instant guidance as to the whereabouts of the topic, and indeed seeing it featuring in different areas can help to focus your choice.

One teacher's experience is an example of this. Initially, as she considered that several pupils were underachieving, Anne set out to study motivation. Later, as a result of scanning some texts, however, she decided that what she *really* wanted to look at was the effect of the teacher's expectations on the pupils' learning. This was as a result of reading about the claimed relationship between the two variables, 'higher expectations' and 'improved perform-ance'. She then concentrated on reading in this narrower field. She also became convinced that it was her own personal responsibility to alter her classroom behaviour rather than change curriculum content or provide extrinsic rewards to stimulate pupil achieve-ment. The literature had helped her clarify her thinking and indicated what kind of action she could take. For her action, she consciously raised her expectations for a group of pupils by giving them 'harder work'. In addition she explained to them in a very positive way that they could meet this challenge. She also made sure that the pupils, with some effort, had enough resources to be successful. She constantly offered reinforcement and encourage-ment but the pupils had to stay with the task and complete it themselves. For evaluation she monitored the effect of her actions on the pupils' work process and progress.

Stage 2: Selecting Key Texts
The second stage is selecting a small number of key texts which are intimately concerned with the refined topic. These tell what other authors and researchers have studied, what questions they asked, what arguments they presented, what methods of investigation they used, i.e. what the up-to-minute state of knowledge about the

topic is. In comparing and contrasting findings from more than one text, the new researchers can critically analyse what has gone before and start the new investigation from an informed and justified base. Additionally, the bibliography in the key texts can source further information for specific topics.

In some investigations, all of the reading can be done before the research action takes place. In most others however, particularly in those based on research questions which are likely to be amended as the research proceeds, it will be necessary to continue consulting the texts during the action to gather information about the change. Retrospective reading after the action may also help to throw light on what was or was not discovered. There is no hard and fast rule, for different reading patterns suit different investigations.

As the research topic gradually crystalises, it can be helpful to think of questions which need to be answered and use these to structure the reading. Again examples taken from teachers who have tried this process may help. The texts which proved very useful are listed in the bibliography.

Example 1: **Creativity**

Graeme wished to explore the area of creativity. He suspected that his present classroom organisation i.e. having specific times for creative writing and creative movement was not conducive to either fostering the creative process or encouraging creative products. He was also interested to find out much more about creativity in children. His first scanning of the library found him surprised that so many writings on the topic of creativity existed and to structure and refine his search he formulated the following questions:-

- What is creativity?
- Can children be creative?
- How can the teacher encourage the creative process?
- What classroom organisation can help?

B

As a result he focussed on selected key texts which particularly concerned creativity and children. The answer to the first question, showing that creativity was not something 'magical and mysterious' but 'an aspect of development which could be improved like any other'(Abbs 1988), gave Graeme the confidence that teaching in this field could help every child, not just a few who possessed a special gift. The second, detailing criteria for a created product gave him pause for thought and caused him to reconsider his terminology. In evaluating the children's work in relation to their stage of development he now anticipated work which was imaginative, new (to them) and self-expressive i.e. expressing their feelings and emotions rather than art-expressive i.e. expressing the art form. And so the literature had firstly assured him that all children could benefit and secondly given him realistic criteria to apply to children's work.

His second two questions concerned the creative process. The literature (Wallas 1980) explained the four stages of the creative process to be 'identifying a problem, incubation, illumination and verification'. The fact that the incubation process was described as slow and lengthy reinforced Graeme's unease that creative writing could happen immediately after a taught input and as a result he used this time for discussion with the children so that they might have a stimulus and a bank of ideas to consider for their creative work at a later date. And by forgetting deadlines for the finished work, he removed the tension which had resulted from the emphasis on the created product diminishing the conditions which fostered a creative process. This guidance from the literature gave Graeme the confidence to proceed. He could justify the reduction of importance on the created product and found after some time that the children were no longer afraid to experiment because they no longer anticipated 'failing' to meet product demands.

Example 2: Raising pupils' self-esteem

Lynn had some pupils from disadvantaged backgrounds who lacked confidence. She saw this in their general demeanour and in their reluctance to participate in group activities. She wished to raise their self-esteem, anticipating that this would help them in class. Lynn explained that she "only had a vague idea about self-esteem" so she noted some questions to guide her literature search. They were -

- What is self-esteem?
- What benefits can pupils gain if their self-esteem is raised?
- Is it realistic to expect that I can raise the self-esteem of these pupils?
- If so, what kind of action can I take?

In formulating these questions Lynn was asking the literature to give an explanation of what the topic was about, a justification for selecting this topic for her pupils in her classroom and some guidance for a possible action. Interestingly, it was this last request which provided most excitement and challenge.

Lynn explained,

"I had more or less anticipated what the answers to the first two questions would be, although the literature of course offered succinct and well written definitions. I wasn't sure about the realism of what I was trying to do but the literature gave me confidence that I could raise the self-esteem of these pupils if I didn't expect change overnight. It also alerted me to the effect other people had and I thought I might explain to one of the boy's mothers (who comes to PTA meetings) what I was trying to do, and she could try to support the idea at home. The fascinating thing was the recommendation in Felker's research (reported by Peter Gurney). It gave five principles for developing self-reward-ing behaviour, and helped me decide on an action".

The principles were,

1. * Adults praise yourselves.

2 Help children to evaluate realistically.

3. Teach children to set reasonable goals.

4. * Teach children to praise themselves.

5. Teach children to praise others.

Lynn's first action concerned Nos.1.and 4 only. She decided to act as a model - she told the children by word and deed that she was proud of being a teacher and proud of her class and, specially conscious of her non-verbal behaviour, she 'walked tall'. Another important change in her practice was to take time to summarise for the pupils what they had achieved by asking "What new things have we done today? What do we know today that we didn't know yesterday? Haven't we done well?" She expected to tackle the other principles in turn and anticipated that they would follow reasonably easily if the first action was successful.

Examples of questions which have been used to structure literature searches:

Example 2: Topic: Problem-solving
- What is problem-solving?
- What abilities and skills are required?
- What techniques do pupils use to solve problems?
- Can successful techniques be shared?
- Does success in one kind of problem-solving activity transfer to other situations?

Example 3: Topic: Drug abuse
- What are the parameters which distinguish between use, misuse and abuse of drugs?
- Are certain groups of pupils more likely to use drugs than others? What factors cause this?
- What drugs are most commonly used by pupils?
- Can an awareness/health education programme prevent pupils becoming drug users?

Example 4: Topic: Integration of pupils with visual impairment
- What is visual impairment?
- What resources will the local authority provide?
- Once the environment is safe, what level of impairment will allow the children to cope?
- Do these children develop coping strategies of their own? What are they?

NB If the research is to be reported, either to other researchers or to a funding body or as a thesis, then it is important for the researcher to keep exact details of all the literature which contributed to the thinking behind the research so that it can be shown in the bibliography of the report. Careful referencing of all the quotations, discussions and conclusions must occur. This allows the readers to have access to the original works and also shows that the researchers are being meticulous in differentiating between the work of others and their own. Failure to do this could result in a charge of plagiarism.

▼▼▼Planning the action in action research

As the research question is clarified, the critical question becomes "What action can I take to gather evidence to answer the research question, or test the hypothesis?"Very often as the preparatory reading and thinking is done, the action to improve the situation becomes easier to plan. This is because the literature actually suggests what could usefully be done. However, other parameters specific to the research context have to be considered if the work is to be completed while all the participants are interested and 'fresh'. The extent of any action will depend on the amount of time the researcher has available, the number of subjects taking part and the implicit time-span i.e. the length of time required for the particular change to happen and for any improvement to occur. (Remember, the action is planned to bring about an improvement).

The action must be carefully organised in advance for classroom interruptions can alter the behaviour of children being observed or cause pupil recordings to be rushed.This may mean that the data is less useful because it does not reflect a true picture of events.

Each piece of action-research will have its own planning issues. The researcher needs to consider the following questions:-

- *What?*
- *` How?*
- *When?*
- *Where?*
- *With whom?*

- *What resources?*
- *What recordings will be made?*
- *What implications?*
- *Who needs to be informed?*
- *Will this action provide evidence to answer the research question?*

- *What?* - What will the action consist of? Will it concern one curriculum area or be a cross-curricular study?

- *How?* - What research strategy will be used? What measures will be taken to reduce bias? What literature will underpin the study? Will the children be told they are taking part? (Consider the implications if they are and if they are not told).

- *When?* - Once per week or more often? At the same or different times each week? (Consider the possibility of the children being tired or restless). Are extra-curricular activities likely to disturb the plan?

- *Where?* - In the classroom or in a quiet area? (Consider the implications of moving the pupils). Are there distractions e.g. school lunches being set up or parents arriving in school? Is there a plug for a tape-recorder? Is the interview area sufficiently private?

- *With whom?* - What children will participate and how will they be selected? Will other adults be involved, perhaps to cover while a few children take part or to make their own observations which will be used to substantiate the research findings and claims?

- *What resources?* - Will questionnaires/interview schedules/ observation schedules need to be prepared in advance? Is a tape-recorder available at the required times? Is the microphone sufficiently strong to record children's voices from the necessary distance? Is there a box for the collection of the completed questionnaires? Do the respondents know where this will be held?

- *What recordings will be made?* - Field notes - where, when and how much detail will need to be recorded? Observations - how often, how much detail, what aspects of non-verbal behaviour? Questionnaire and interview responses - how are they to be analysed?

- *What implications?* - If the findings are important, and point to certain things being required or certain changes needing to be made, is the climate such that they can happen?

- *Who needs to be informed?* - Do the parents have to give permission? Would it be courteous to let the headteacher and teachers holding promoted posts know the proposed action plans?

- *Will this action provide evidence to answer the research question/test the hypothesis?* - Is the research tightly structured without distractions?

If some of the children in the class are not to be involved in the research, then their time must be organised too....with equally absorbing activities to save them being resentful and/or disruptive while the research proceeds.

The action itself may be proceeded by an information gathering exercise. The pupils may complete a questionnaire or have an interview asking about, e.g. their knowledge of or attitude to the subject of the investigation so that the teacher can plan the most appropriate action or select the most appropriate children for the study. (For information about questionnaires and interviews see Chapter 3). Alternatively, or in addition questionnaires or interviews may follow the 'action' perhaps to monitor the increase in pupils' understanding or to find what changes in attitude have occurred over the duration of the investigation. A questionnaire can also be used to allow the pupils to evaluate what has occurred. But these pre and post action strategies do not usually count as the 'action'. The action is a planned move to improve a situation, not only an information gathering activity.

If time is short or if the research is really planned to monitor the effect of the action on just a few pupils, then *they* can form a group and the research can be confined to them. Alternatively, the research action can include the whole class but the data gathering and analysis need only involve the few. This is quite a useful strategy as it avoids the chosen group feeling special or picked on and altering their behaviour accordingly. Later, when time is favourable or if someone else can help with the data analysis then the extra data from the other pupils can provide interest and additional information. These are the kinds of considerations which need to be planned in advance.

N.B. Above all the action must be planned so that evidence to answer the research question or test the hypothesis can be gathered. It is all too easy to go off at a tangent. Researchers should constantly ask themselves "if I find _____ or _____ , will this answer the research question or test the hypothesis?" If the answer is 'no' then some re-thinking is vital.

▼▼▼Reducing bias in action research

Bias is the name given to anything which distorts i.e. anything which prevents a true picture of events being recorded.

PERSONAL (i.e. caused by the researcher).

BIAS   <

PROCEDURAL (i.e. caused by the research methods).

Action-research carried out by teachers in their own class-rooms can be particularly open to accusations of bias because the participants in the research have built-in expectations of one another. These may prevent objective measures being made and thus cloud the real outcomes. Additionally, even in classrooms where the teacher/pupil relationship is open and friendly, some residual power structure (i.e. the pupils seeing the teacher/re-searcher as someone in authority) may prevent the pupils record-ing their true feelings. What then, can teachers/researchers do to try to reduce the bias implicit in a personal interaction?

Personal Bias

1.Consider cues
Teachers have to be aware that their appearance (traditional - trendy), their attitudes (authoritarian - laissez faire), their practices

(e.g. cycling to school, smoking at intervals) are quickly picked up by the pupils. This can be seen when pupils imitate mannerisms the teachers don't even realise they have! The point is that pupils are likely to make assumptions on the basis of these observations and these may cause them to alter their responses e.g. pupils aware of the teacher's stance on green issues or peace issues or vegetarianism from discussions or even just from stickers on the teacher's car are more likely to give the kinds of responses they think the teacher wants to hear. Of course, pupils may wish to 'get back at' the teacher and so support the opposite point of view.

In these cases the research is not measuring the pupils' own attitudes free of any contaminating influence. This kind of bias can be reduced by the teacher assuring the pupils that different people have different views which are all important or by having some class debates before the research where the 'pros and cons' of a selection of debatable issues are given the same respectful hearing. In addition, teachers must think through the process of explaining the research to the pupils (e.g. will their manner of presentation or tone of voice or posture give unspoken messages to the pupils?) and be aware of the implications of their stance.

2. Involve other observers

Personal bias can be particularly apparent in claims made from observations. It is particularly hard, for example, for teachers who have spent much time and energy preparing activities to motivate reluctant learners to admit that their pupils remain unmoved! Anxious that the pupils should have a better experience, the teachers, even unconsciously, tend to see what they want to see. One way of overcoming this is to *gather evidence from other sources* e.g. by asking other teachers to be observers. In this case an observation schedule (see P59) which contains enough information for the observer to record independent judgements is a useful tool. Another strategy (e.g. to monitor motivation) is to consider the work that the children have produced since the action in terms of both quantity and quality and to compare that to pre-research days. Another possibility would be video recording events pre and post action. Having different recorders or recording instruments is a very sound research tool - one called triangulation.

Fig. 3   Motivating Martin

Procedural bias

1. Selecting Subjects

If the purpose of the research is to monitor the effect of the research action on specific pupils (and remember it has been planned to provide some kind of improvement for them), then these pupils are the research subjects and the report is likely to be in the form of Case Studies which would portray a very detailed background to let the readers understand the context. The findings would say 'This occurred for these pupils in this context over a period of .... weeks'. No claims to generalisation (i.e. that this would occur for all pupils) would be made. If, however, the teachers wished to monitor their own competence or effectiveness in doing something e.g. developing discussion skills, then they would be short-sighted to choose pupils who were willing or able discussants because success would as likely be due to the pupils' experience and ability as much as improved teaching. A random selection of pupils or the choice of a mixed ability group could avert the charge of the results being biased. The results could also be affected if one group was not used to working together because then, reluctance to contribute could arise from the pupils not knowing how their peer group would receive their efforts. Some group activities i.e. familiarisation time, could overcome this. The implications of all sorts of decisions must be considered in advance of the action.

2. Anonymity: Confidentiality.
One measure which can effectively reduce bias is to offer the respondents anonymity or confidentiality. The assurance that no-one else will know their responses is to try to persuade them to make 'honest' replies. If they do not anticipate any disagreement or reprisal they are more likely to tell the truth! Anonymity can be promised if the researchers genuinely do not know who the subjects are e.g. who is completing the questionnaire. If the results *are* identifiable in some way, (and researchers who wish to follow up any non-returners to get a higher response rate generally mark the questionnaires to allow them to do this), then the respondents can only be assured of confidentiality. Once the assurances have been made, it goes without saying that they should be kept. It can seem absurd to offer pupils anonymity when they know full well that the teacher will recognise their writing. In this case the pupils could either print their responses or another adult could collate them onto one blank questionnaire which would then be returned to the class teacher. This could be explained to the pupils.

3. Reliability
If all possible measures are taken to reduce bias in the collection of data then researchers can claim that they have aimed for reliability - i.e. the state which would exist if another researcher carried out the investigation in the same situation and came up with the same results. Reliability results from being objective, i.e. rigorous in planning, in carrying out the research and in recording and analysing the data.

▼▼▼**Defining the research population**

In any research where generalisation *is* to be claimed, then it is important that a random selection of the population concerned with the research is consulted. To determine the research population, the question "Who are the people who will be affected by the results?" needs to be answered.

If, for example, the school wanted an up-to-date report of parents' views on whether school uniform should be worn, then a random selection of all parents in the school community would need to be consulted. Whether the proportion was 'the parents of every 5th pupil on the register' or 'the parents of every 20th pupil' would depend on the resources (time/money) available to the researchers, the size of the school, or whether both parents or guardians were being consulted separately. If the school, however, only wished to know the views of parents who had more than two children, or of parents who were unemployed then these specific groups could form the research population and a random sample would be taken from them.

The researchers have to be clear in their mind *exactly* what they want to know and this clarifies the parameters of the research population. An example may clarify this procedure.

Example of a process to help define a research population

Research Topic:

A survey of local opinion to help with the planning of a weekly activities afternoon to be held in the school's Community Wing.

Research Strategy:

A questionnaire distributed to (? Population) to ask members of the community whether they would be likely to participate in community activities on a regular basis, if so what activities they would like to have and (because the grant is small) whether they would be prepared to pay (daily? weekly? monthly?) for these activities.

Resources:

Cash is very tight. The accommodation is free but heating and lighting have to be paid for and materials for the activities have to be supplied, therefore some charge has to be made. The cost of printing and distributing the questionnaires will also have to be met from entrance fees.

Defining the research population:
i.e. People who are to receive the questionnaire.

Questions to be considered:
? Every family in the neighbourhood? If not, what radius constitutes the neighbourhood?
? Householders where occupants are elderly? If not, what will the cut-off age be?
? Householders where both partners are known to work in the afternoon?
? Only parents of children who attend *this* school? What of people who have no children?
? Children (the session begins at 3.45pm). What age groups? Would crèche facilities be a good thing?
? Families temporarily out of the district?
? Only families who usually participate in community activities?

This list is not exhaustive. Each question leads on to others. It just shows the pre-planning which is necessary if the correct population is to be identified. This kind of preparation helps the researcher justify the population that is chosen and helps avert claims of bias, or worse still wasted resources, due to the 'wrong groups' or 'restricted groups' being chosen to take part in the research, in this case to receive the questionnaires.

If interviews are to be used, then the selection of interviewees is very important. They should again be the result of random selection rather than people who are known to have clear views and who can talk forcefully! As there are likely to be fewer interviews (due to time/cost considerations) than questionnaire replies, then it is very important that the people chosen are representative of the research population.

In interviews within classroom action-research, interviewees may by chosen because of their specialist knowledge of the topic (e.g. the P.E. teacher in Jean's research on motor impairment), or because of their willingness to be involved. This would be reported in the same way as the selection of children for Case Studies i.e. with detailed explanation of why this was done.

3

Gaining access to respondents

In all research, and particularly in research involving children, it is important that researchers plan how best to gain access to their respondents. They cannot take it for granted that people will be willing or able to participate in their study.

In schools children appear to be ideal subjects. They attend regularly, they are divided into age groups and may be sub-divided into other smaller groups. Much of the research organisation is already done. The children themselves are usually willing to be involved in something new and are lively, humourous participants, unlikely or unable to say 'No'! But this makes them vulnerable, even open to exploitation and there may be very good reasons why they should not be involved. Researchers have to have the permission of the teacher, the head teacher and possibly the parents. This is unlikely to be problematic if teachers are researchers in their own classrooms and especially if they are attempting to improve an aspect of their teaching, however it is better to share ideas and make sure that no recriminations arise once the research is underway.

If other teachers, parents, social workers or people in the community *are* to be involved, access may be more difficult. Certainly headteachers will need to know who is to be approached and the envisaged scale of the involvement. They are likely to ask what the purpose of the study will be, how long it will take and they will certainly request a preview of any questionnaire, interview or observation schedule. They may also want to know when the results will be reported.

If teachers wish to enter another school e.g. to gain a larger sample of one age group of pupils, it is extremely important to check out the possibility of access in the early days of conceptualising the research so that the school does not feel pressurised into accepting a procedure which it would rather have refused. If this *does* happen, a slight shift in focus or involving different groups of people could be all that is required. It may be that the school has just finished asking the same questions or that the same children have been targeted for something else - it does not mean that the study is based on a poor idea. Researchers have to anticipate all kinds of snags and show that they are flexible and resilient!

Researchers should reassure their prospective respondents that all information will be treated in confidence and that neither the school nor any child or adult will be identified by name in a final report. A good tactic is to offer to share parts of the text as they are written. This is by no means essential but it can show that the study is not 'about' the children or 'about' the school in any threatening sense. In fact if teachers are being asked to take part, perhaps in discussing questions or in comparing observations or even in taking part in interviews, they often like to see how their contribution appears in the writing up. This sharing gesture can often promote further co-operation.

Planning the approach

Once permission to carry out the research has been granted, there still remains the issue of requesting the co-operation of the subjects. Researchers in classrooms need to consider whether the pupils should be told they are taking part in research, if indeed they have a right to know. The subject of the research may influence this decision. If, for example, the pupils' changing patterns of behaviour are being monitored, or the effects of changed classroom organisation or developments in their social interaction, then probably it would be best for pupils not to know in case a heightened awareness of being observed caused them to alter their behaviour. On the other hand, if the results were to contribute to a larger study eg. pupils' perceptions on Green issues, or if the results could affect the pupils' own lifestyles eg. changing local leisure facilities, then they must know the importance and be able to anticipate the implications of their replies. Researchers have to make these kinds of decisions knowing the topic, the subjects and the contexts, and this reasoning would be reported in the final writing up.

If questionnaires are to be distributed or interviews requested, then a friendly, carefully planned statement explaining the purpose of the research can act as an ice breaker. Two examples follow.

Example 1.

"Thank you very much for taking the time and trouble to complete this questionnaire (or attend this interview). The topic of my research is Parental Involvement and I am trying to find out if parents of P 7 children wish to be involved in school life and if so, what aspects they would prefer to support. The information will be used to help me to make plans so that people can do what they wish to do. All replies are confidential."

This introductory statement should be brief, just covering the main purpose of the research. Explaining the research in context should put potential respondents at their ease and encourage them to participate. Researchers should offer some reciprocation if they can. In this case, it was a hope that prior organisation would enable parents to do what they wished to do if they became involved in school life.

If young children are to be asked questions on sensitive subjects, then a letter to the parents requesting permission is a necessary first step. The following letter is an example.

Example 2.

'Dear (Parent),
In school we are planning a new Health Education programme for Jamie's year group. Before this happens, and to ensure that the material is entirely appropriate, we anticipate carrying out a piece of research based on the following questions.
1. What do the children already know about the harmful effects of smoking and in what ways has this knowledge influenced their intention to smoke?
2. What do the children already know about the use of medicinal drugs taken under supervision to promote health and the misuse of harmful drugs which cause ill health?
And after the programme, we would intend to ask,
3. Do the pupils consider that this new programme has helped them to avoid taking risks with their own health?

The intention is that the children complete two question-naires, one before and one after the programme. To pre-serve confidentiality, another teacher (who cannot identify the children by their writing) will analyse the results. This means that no-one will know what individual children said - only the class results will be used to plan the programme. A copy of the questionnaires will be available in the Secre-tary's room from............, that is two weeks before the research begins. Please contact the Secretary by.............. if you do not wish Jamie to participate.
Thank you,
Yours sincerely
(Researcher)'

Although this kind of approach involves early preparation and extra organisation, it does allow the researcher to proceed with confidence knowing that parents' and pupils' rights have been observed. The purpose of the research was conveyed to the parents along with reciprocation - i.e. that a totally relevant programme would be planned. This prevents any recriminations e.g. that pupils are being 'used for research', and hopefully encourages participation.

One sixteen-year-old girl who had recently left school with no qualifications was asked to complete a lengthy questionnaire about her school experience. The reciprocation offered was that the researchers would use the information to get things better for the *next* cohort of pupils. The lass replied,

"I think you's have got a cheek asking me to fill this in after all you's should have came and told us what to do for the best instead of asking kids lots of things to help other peo-ple"

Source: Tell Them from ME.

I rest my case!

4

Data Gathering Instruments

▼▼▼ Questionnaires

The questionnaire is an effective way of gathering a lot of information from a large number of people..... effective that is, if the questions produce helpful responses!   Although inexperienced researchers may think that this kind of research strategy is relatively straightforward, just 'asking some questions and analysing some replies', it really can be very difficult to conceptualise questions which are clear and unambiguous, which encourage the respondents to reply honestly and which are free of contamination i.e. the response to one question affecting another. But these criteria must be met if the research is to produce meaningful data.   Very often the process can be eased if some research has already been completed on the topic being studied.   In that case the findings can indicate the kinds of questions which could usefully be asked in the new research.

Once the questions have been formulated, the most helpful way forward is to pilot the questionnaire on just a small group of people and study their replies. These can show whether they have readily understood the questions or if they have (mis)interpreted them in unexpected ways.   It is usually very revealing if researchers can study a few completed questionnaires for these immediately show the quality and quantity of information which is likely to be collected in the full scale investigation. There is then time for other questions to be added, unsatisfactory ones to be amended or deleted or for the balance of open and closed questions to be changed. The formulation of 'good' questions, the piloting and the early evaluation is time-consuming but invariably time well spent for nothing can be more frustrating than realising, too late, that other questions would have provided more significant answers.

It can be helpful for the researcher to compile a questionnaire and then leave it aside for some time..... later it can be re-read from the (imaginary) viewpoint of different recipients e.g. a newly redundant father, a single parent, a 'well-off' family, someone with reading difficulties. This exercise can help the researcher to evaluate the clarity and the balance of the questionnaire from a range of different perspectives.

The design of the questionnaire

• *Number of questions*
When considering the number of questions which should be asked, it is helpful to think of the concentration span of the respondents (children probably having fewer questions), the number of lead-in questions necessary to put the respondents at their ease and the number of key questions which provide the critical information. Probably around twenty questions would need to be asked but this will depend on the complexity of each.

• *Purpose of questions*
As each question is prepared the researcher should ask, 'Why do I need to know this?' The answer, 'to find ....' should indicate *if and in what ways the information will illuminate the research question/hypothesis.* If the researcher cannot define the purpose of the question then the question should be reconsidered or modified or omitted. To be valid each question must be tightly tied to the research issue. If the purpose is clear, then later when the questionnaires are returned, the researcher can with confidence ask, 'What have I discovered about ....?' and not be left saying 'What sense can I make of this data?'.

• *Lead-in Questions*
It is important that respondents are put at their ease so that they are encouraged to complete and return the questionnaire. To facilitate this, easier questions are usually asked first. Some researchers however, waste this space by asking for biographical details, e.g. age, sex, address, number in the family, employment status, when this information has nothing to do with the investigation at hand. When these details *are* important, when, for example the research aims to find how well in academic terms 'middle children' do, or if living in high rise flats has affected the participation of ten year old boys in leisure activities, then biographical information on these points is critical. The point is that respondents can quickly become impatient with too many questions especially if they see

them as irrelevant or unnecessarily personal or even threatening. This may affect their concentration or willingness to continue and so it is very important that all the questions should be scrutinised carefully and superfluous items removed.

• *Key Questions*
Different kinds of question add interest, give variety and help to prevent the respondents from replying without reading the question carefully. The design of each question will also affect the kind of response which is given, so it is useful to try to anticipate the amount of detail which is required to enlighten the study and to prepare the kind of question which will stimulate that kind of response.

Closed questions i.e. those having a Yes/No answer e.g.
Do you agree with school uniform?

Yes	No	Don't know
❑	❑	❑

Please tick

Closed with alternatives e.g.
How do you travel to school?

bus	car	walk	train	bicycle
❑	❑	❑	❑	❑

Please tick

Closed with some scale e.g.
What do you think of corporal punishment?

Approve	Neutral	Disapprove
❑	❑	❑

Please tick

How much of the lesson did you enjoy?

All of it	Some of it	None of it
❑	❑	❑

Please tick

Did you find the work

Too difficult	Just about right	Too easy
❑	❑	❑

Please tick

Closed with alternative suggestions e.g.

Please indicate (1,2,3) the three kinds of class activity which you consider to be most helpful and the most enjoyable for you.

	helpful (1,2,3)	enjoyable (1,2,3)
• having notes dictated by the teacher	❏	❏
• having 'stations' and tasks	❏	❏
• having debates and discussion groups	❏	❏
• doing written examples	❏	❏
• researching topics in class	❏	❏
• researching topics outside school	❏	❏
• using listening posts	❏	❏
• using videotapes	❏	❏
• other? Please say what...............	❏	❏

Open Questions e.g.

What do you think of . . . .?
Please write a few lines about . . . . .?

Closed questions can usually be answered quickly because no explanation is required. Open questions provide more qualitative information because the respondents are able to express their feelings in their own words.

Cartoon type questions e.g.

Put a ring around Ralph the Tortoise to show how you feel
1. When its time to do P.E.?

Several lines of Ralph can allow the pupils to record their evaluations about different aspects of any school experience. The light-hearted approach is to help them record their true feelings - thus reducing bias. A sliding scale, recording depth of feeling is implicit in the drawings.

Questionnaires and bias

The questionnaire asks a number of people standardised questions in the same order. In most cases, there is no face-to-face interaction and the respondents are free to ignore any question or in fact not to return the questionnaires. There is no time pressure to complete the document and so there is time and opportunity for the respondents to reflect on the responses they have made and to change or extend them. Moreover, the replies are confidential. These are all measures which can effectively reduce bias in the collection of data.

An element of bias remains, however, in the selection of questions (why has this question been chosen, not others?). To attempt to overcome this, the questions should ensure that disparate, graded or alternative views can be recorded. For example, in a questionnaire on stress factors, the question:

	Yes	No
• Does ---------- cause you stress at work?	☐	☐

would contain less potential bias if it was presented thus:

In most work places ----------- is present.
Does this cause you;

	Yes	No
• No anxiety at all?	☐	☐
• Some anxiety at times?	☐	☐
• Stress but you cope?	☐	☐
• Sometimes an unacceptable level of stress?	☐	☐
• Distress - so that you feel unable to cope?	☐	☐
• Distress - so that you become ill?	☐	☐
• Distress so that you have seriously considered resigning?	☐	☐

• Would you like to say more? -----------------------------------
----

In this mode, the recipient is alerted to a range of alternative feelings and so can provide a more personal and meaningful account about the effects of stress.

A final point concerning questionnaires and bias is that the respondents themselves may bias the sample. If, for example, a larger group from middle class homes than working class homes reply then the results are not truly reflecting the group who were equally represented in the original sample.

• *Language*
The language used should be user-friendly i.e. free of terminology and suitable for the group of respondents being consulted.

• *Anticipating the analysis*
Broadly speaking, the closed questions are easier to analyse but they do result in *data degradation* i.e. loss of relevant and important information.   This is because the respondents cannot record their depth of feeling or any explanation of what caused them to make that response.   Because of this, results from the closed questions can only produce descriptions not explanations, e.g. - 30% of respondents considered that the School Board had done a good job. On the other hand, open-ended questions can give the respondents the opportunity to explain their reply, e.g. The School Board led the protest against the amalgamation with ----- ---- effectively because........ With open questions however, the respondents may have difficulty in communicating their thoughts clearly.   This leads to difficulties in analysing the results.   A balance of enough guidance to show exactly what is wanted and enough freedom to allow the respondents to record other important details is ideal!

Organisation: Distribution and Collection

'Getting them out and getting them in' needs careful planning too. The following questions can guide the preparation.

• *What method of distribution?* A postal questionnaire usually has a S.A.E. to encourage respondents to reply. Questionnaires may also be taken home by pupils if they are likely to deliver

- *How many should be sent out?* Knowing the research population and the importance of the content to them may give the researcher some idea of the likely returner-rate . . . . usually 60% is a favourable return. The number of responses is important for the credibility of the analysis of data and for any subsequent claims which are to be made.

- *What length of time should the respondents have for completing and returning the questionnaires?* Usually ten days is a favourable time span, i.e. long enough for very busy but willing respondents and not long enough for the documents to be lost. Postal questionnaires obviously take longer than pupil-dependent ones but they may be safer.

- *Timing of Distribution?* Sometimes, to find the best time, it can be useful to consider the lifestyle of the recipients. 'Just before the summer holidays' might be a good time for the researchers as they anticipate some free time when they can concentrate on the analysis of the data, but holiday preparations may prevent the recipients completing the questionnaires. And similarly 'just before Christmas', the important envelope may be lost in the flood of advertising materials which invades many homes.

  There may also be 'sensitive' times in the school year, e.g. when pupil reports have newly gone home! It could be better to avoid these times if questions to do with the curriculum or the effects of changing organisation are to be asked, in case achievement or non-achievement contaminates the replies!

  These timing considerations may influence the number of replies and therefore the quantity and quality of the analysis which can be made. This in turn must affect the claims to generalisation, and so the impact of the findings may be considerably reduced.

- *Should questionnaires be coded? What is to happen if 'enough' replies fail to come in?   Should reminders be sent?* If the decision is 'Yes', then the researchers need to know who has already replied.   Coding against addresses has to be organised before the initial distribution and replies have to be 'marked off' as they appear. This involves extra organisation but it can result in a higher response rate being achieved. The researchers have to remember to promise confidentiality not anonymity if this is the case.

• *Collection Point?* A safe box in the Secretary's room can allow postal replies to be stored and pupil-returned replies to be deposited anonymously if this is important to the study.   A mark on the outside of the return envelope can let the Secretary know what is inside. This   saves returns being mistakenly distributed to other parts of the building and then being lost. Competent organisation is essential!

The results of questionnaires

The results may be displayed as percentages in a table or on an exemplar of the actual questionnaire. The former is usual if the results of only one or two questions are being considered; the latter is helpful if all the questions are being used. The writing which accompanies the tables, diagrams (e.g. bar charts or pie charts) will explain what the percentages mean and explain the possible implications of the results. In the appendix, a few examples of completed questionnaires give authenticity i.e. they show that the research was undertaken and that different people responded. It is particularly enlightening if different answers to the same questions form part of the illustration, particularly if these concern claims made in the Review of Literature or if they are central in answering the research question. Other completed questionnaires should be retained even if they are not included in the final report (apart from the results affecting the analysis) - just in case further clarification or extra evidence is requested.

Summary
And so questionnaires can ask a large number of people a number of pre-set questions. They are standardised. They are answered in the same order. There is no face-to-face interaction and so no interviewer bias. Questions, however, cannot be altered during the course of the research and in analysis frustration can arise through data degradation. Researchers have no real control over the response rates, and the number/type of respondents who do reply may bias the sample.

▼▼▼ Interviews

The interview is a face-to-face interaction which allows the interviewer to ask *prepared questions* and in addition *to probe* the respondent so that further information is obtained. The respondent has the opportunity to explain why the replies are as they are and the interviewer, through noting non-verbal cues and factors such as the time between the question and the reply, can also record assessments of 'strength of feeling' or 'reluctance to reply'. The interviewee has also some freedom to expand on issues or to ask for clarification of a question or to put questions back in the interviewer's court.

• *Interview Bias*
While this research strategy is advantageous in gaining more qualitative information, the interviewer must be aware of all the sources of bias and try to reduce their influence. In any meeting or interaction, the two people immediately begin to make assumptions about each other and these can influence their responses. In an interview the respondent may be influenced by the interviewer's age, dress, manner and competence in handling the procedure as well as the choice of topic being studied. And if that was not enough, the interviewer's own opinions may be deduced (either accurately or inaccurately) through voice intonation and non-verbal behaviour!

Aware of the difficulties, however, researchers can take steps to reduce this bias. A useful first move can be for potential interviewers to practise the interview technique with friends, asking them to note behaviours which give clues as to the researcher's stance on the topic being studied. The next step is to try to reduce these behaviours - easier said than done.....but essential if the interviewer is to be relaxed and confident and able to concentrate on the interviewee!

Preparing the questions in advance and staying with the prepared plan is another good ploy. Then researchers can avoid having to think up questions as the interview proceeds and perhaps even unintentionally leading or pressurising the respondent into replying in a particular way. It is very difficult to retrieve an interview i.e. to get 'honest' replies once the respondent has gauged the interviewer's reaction to the answers as more or less favourable.

The probes also need planning. "Would you say a little more about that" is less emotive than "Gracious, tell me more" or "Well, that's surprising.....go on....!" Generally speaking, the interviewer should introduce the topic and then try to intervene as little as possible. A proficient interviewer can use silences or phatics (mmm...) or facial expressions....i.e. different strategies which will encourage the interviewee to proceed. This is good practice, for the interview is not a chat or a discussion, it is a prepared opportunity to elicit the views of the interviewee and the explanations of why these views are held.

And so, interviewers must be able to encourage people who won't talk, quell others who won't stop and re-route others who go off at a tangent. An interview is not likely to be successful if the interviewer only prays for inspiration on the day!

• *Number of Questions*
As with the questionnaire, thought must be given to the number of questions which will determine the length of the interview. It is a good idea to tell the interviewee in advance that the interview is likely to last a certain time, say 15-20 mins, so that pre-knowledge can prevent any irritation due to the interview taking too long or too short a time! While the complexity of the topic will determine the number of questions, the experience of the interviewer must also be taken into account! A short to-the-point interview is likely to yield data which is vital and fresh, while a protracted interview can lack dynamism and become tedious.

At the start of the interview, pleasantries can help the interviewee to relax as can a brief prepared explanation (in user friendly language) of what the interview is about. Assurances of confidentiality should be made early along with thanks to the interviewee for being prepared to participate. The interviewer must aim for a courteous, relaxed interaction. The interviewee must go away feeling that views and explanations have been valued and recorded accurately.

• *Types of Questions*
All questions must be clear and unambiguous as in the questionnaire. While the interviewee does have the opportunity to ask for clarification or explanation, reluctance to do this due to embarrassment or nervousness or even just hesitation can mean that any

misunderstanding can be passed over. If this happens and if, as a result of this, the interviewer does not fully understand the response, the whole quality of the interview is in jeopardy.

While the interviewer remains in control for nearly all of the time, the interviewee may wish to elaborate an issue or describe a related issue. The interviewer should allow space for this asking e.g. Are there other questions you would like to ask or issues you would like to raise? The skilled interviewer knows that listening can be as important as questioning provided the talk is closely related to the topic at hand.

• *Statements*
Another strategy is for the interviewer to read statements to the interviewee and ask for the degree of agreement or disagreement which the statement invokes. Ostensibly the statement 'comes from other people' and so reduces bias in the form of the interviewee's reluctance to disagree with the interviewer, the power figure in the interchange. Dillon's (1988) work has shown that statements can be more provocative than questions which can inhibit the respondent. The example on p.55 of an Interview Schedule is based on statements. An interesting interview could combine both strategies.

• *Organisation*
Times of interviews are arranged ahead of the day of action. If researchers can know the whereabouts of interviewees prior to the interview, they can be contacted if last minute hitches prevent it taking place. The interviewee may be prepared to give a contact phone number if this kind of explanation (i.e. emergency use only) is given.

The setting for the interview is important. A degree of comfort and privacy is essential. If the interview is to be tape-recorded, then it goes without saying that an interviewer must be proficient in this skill. Nothing is more off-putting to the interviewee than to be halted mid-stream because the machine is not recording properly, and to be asked to start again! It can also be very distracting if the interviewer's eyes are constantly checking levels of recording or whether there is enough tape left to record the whole interview! All the technicalities must be checked out before the interviewee arrives if the researcher is to have credibility.

- *Time Management*

If interviews are sequentially arranged, it is better to leave a more than adequate time gap between each. This allows for late arrivals, loquacious participants and resetting the tape-recorder. Interviewers will also wish to check that they have recorded *all* the vital information i.e. including non-verbal cues which will not appear on the tape-recording, and so time for field notes should be allowed. And finally, interviewing is exhausting. Taking time to recharge.....i.e. batteries *and* brains is a very necessary part of surviving to tell the tale.

- *Number of Interviews*

The time-consuming nature of the interview process means that, unless there are several researchers involved, only a few interviews can be held. The richness of the data with descriptions, explanations, justifications and additions from the interviewee's own experience should compensate for the much smaller number of replies.

- *Anticipating the Analysis*

Analysing qualitative data is a very slow process involving transcribing tapes and interpreting the dialogue. Researchers should plan the number of interviews and the length of each in the knowledge that a lengthy procedure of analysis lies ahead.

Interview Schedules

These schedules (which may be held by the interviewer during the interview like the market researcher on the street corner) can be helpful in

- acting as an aide-memoire for the researcher;

- letting the interviewee know that care has been taken in preparation, that a number of questions have to be covered and that the responses will be carefully noted.

Example:
Interview schedule. Topic: *Parents' evaluations of School Boards*

Interviewer begins,
   "I have a number of statements gathered from groups of Parents who have served on different School Boards. It would be helpful to know whether you feel the same way about your experience. Please say if you agree or disagree, if you are not sure, or if you would like to add you own views on the topic."

	Agrees	Disagrees	Don't know	Other response
1.The school has welcomed the formation of the School Board and has provided support and information to allow it to function properly.				
2.The composition of Parents on the Board is not representative of the children in the school.				
3.The advice given by the Board has been acted upon.				
4.The headteacher and members of staff are the most powerful people in the group. Other members are influenced by their decisions to an unacceptable extent.				
5. The Parents on the Board are really only concerned with what will affect their own children.				

Alternatively the researcher might prefer to ask the questions in a less formal way e.g. "I wonder if you would like to tell me about being a member of the School Board?". In this situation the interviewee could well cover aspects not on the interview schedule, however if the points 1 - 5 form the crux of the interview, the interviewer should anticipate the subsequent interaction and know how to (tactfully) elicit the required information.

Analysing data from interviews

If you have been permitted to record your interviews, then you probably have a great deal of information which has to be transcribed. Rather than transcribing the entire interview, listen carefully to the tape and extract episodes which are particularly relevant i.e. which provide information concerning the research question or hypothesis. Transcribe these carefully. Alongside the conversation you could include some information (see Example 1) which will help the reader to understand your analysis of the conversation...(This is not essential. You would need to transcribe quickly while the interview is fresh in your mind or alternatively make field notes on your interview schedule.) In addition, you could usefully give actual quotations in the text. These can also help to preserve the atmosphere of the interview (Example 2). Be sure to say whether the examples are reflecting several responses or if they are unusual. This helps the reader interpret the analysis accurately.

Example 1	*I= Interviewer R= Respondent*	
Non Verbal Cues		*Transcription*
	I:	Would you like to tell me?
Hesitation		
	R:	Well, I don't know
Silence		
	I:	Would you like to say a little more...?
Moves forward, very tense		
	R:	Certainly not...but I'll explain...
Relaxes back in chair		
	I:	Uh - huh - - and so - ?
Giving information readily.	R:	The main point as I see it is ...

Example 2
In a project on transition from P7 - S1, several pupils spoke of their fears of going to - - - High School. Mary's reply was typical. She explained *"I'm worried about getting lost and all they bullies in the playground. They take things and hit you."*

N.B.
If the research is to be reported as a dissertation or thesis, then guidance on the amount of the transcription required needs to be sought from the particular Institution making the award.

▼▼▼ Observation Schedules

Observation schedules are a very useful means of recording objective evidence and as such can reduce the possibility of collecting biased data. They can be used at different stages in the research. Early on they may assist teachers in choosing a research problem or topic because the schedules can show whether the teachers' self-appraisals (through reflection on current practice) are accurate and justified. It can be very difficult for teachers to accurately gauge the effectiveness of their teaching and to decide what to do first. When the Flanders Interaction Analysis Category (F.I.A.C.) was used to measure the type and quantity of classroom interaction, many if not most teachers were amazed to discover the high proportion of 'teacher talk' which characterised their lessons. And so an observation schedule which is a structured process can give an accurate picture of what is happening in a classroom and be used as a basis for selecting a research topic. Indeed several schedules recorded sequentially could form a useful record of progress towards the anticipated goal.

Observation schedules can be completed by friendly colleagues on a peer-appraisal basis. Obviously decisions about what aspect of teaching has to be observed and recorded have to be discussed in advance to determine e.g. how often the recordings should be made and what coding system should be used. Two examples follow. Karen used one kind of schedule to clarify her self-appraisal, Tony used another to assess the children's competence in discussion.

c

Example 1. Topic: Communication   Teacher: Karen
Karen tells of her experience;
"I had just managed to get the integrated day going - the idea being that the children worked at their own pace and had more responsibility for organising their own activities. You know what it's like, trying to juggle all the groups and making sure the early finishers keep working. I got very tense and the atmosphere in the class changed... I could sense it but I wasn't sure why. Luckily (or so it seems now anyway!), Jim, a teacher I know well was teaching in the next bay. He was more experienced than I was - he ran the integrated day smoothly - and I thought I was following the same pattern, but the whole effort was getting me down.

When we eventually discussed this he listened 'over the wall' as it were, and came to the conclusion that I was so tied up with the organisation that I had turned into a nag. Naturally he didn't say that, but that's what he meant. I had anticipated every possible disaster and my organisation had turned into a series of Don't do this...don't do that! Don't waste time...don't rush all at once to collect the books...don't go on to artwork till you have completed your maths etc. etc. etc. I expect you can imagine! I was reluctant to believe Jim at first but when I thought back over the lessons I could hear myself going on and on...but I couldn't stop because there were so many pitfalls to avoid. As a result of all of this I decided that I must be much more positive in my approach, so I went back to the drawing board and thought how I could turn negative incidents around to make them into positive ones. I also had to believe that the pupils were capable of managing the organisation and somehow convey that to them...I had to build a trust relationship.

This was much harder than anything I'd tried before, however I did believe it would be a lifesaver if I could get it right...and Jim was there with suggestions and was prepared to watch and help me so we devised an observation schedule. I had the idea from College when I'd observed children on an 'on-task/off-task' basis . And so, when this piece of research came along, it was a real opportunity to grasp the nettle and find the differences that striving to be positive made to my teaching.

*Knowing I was being watched did affect my teaching be-
haviour - I was specially conscious of repeating things I'd
set out to avoid, but the fact that the schedule recorded
'improvements' i.e. positive interactions, as well as the
residual negative ones helped. Jim says I can do the same for
him, as soon as he can think of something he's not good at!!"*

Observation schedule

		Positive Verbal	Positive N.V.	Negative Verbal	Negative N.V.	
Group	1	✔ ✔✔	○ ✔ ✔ Anne			Tuesday 9.15 - 9.45 Recording 9.15 - 9.30
	2	✔ ✔	✔ ✔○ Graeme	✗		
	3	○ ③ Sacha		✗ ✔ ✔ Colin	✗ Colin	
Group	1	✔ ② Peter	✔ ○		✔	11.45- 12.15 Recording 12.00 - 12.15
	2	✔ ○ ○ Lyn	✔ ✔	○ ○ ○ ○ Colin Ian	✔ ✔ ✔	
	3	✔ ① Jane		✔ ✔	✗ ✗ ✗ ✗ Colin Colin Alan Colin	

Topic: Communication.

✓ General
○ Direct to one pupil
✗ Repetition of same instruction (negative)
○ Good effort-remember this - e.g.
① 'You organised the painting well yesterday, see if you can do it again.'
② Everyone has finished because there has been no time wasting.
③ It's great to know how well you can plan your time chart.

The two teachers compiled the schedule to suit their own particular needs. They found that 2x15 minute sessions was the optimum time to make the observations i.e. during the early period, "when it was easier to hang on to prepared comments" and just before lunch, "when the children were restless and all the finishing up had to be organised."

What the teachers had not anticipated and what emerged was that a pattern of each group's experience was recorded. Group 3 was having a poor time of it largely due to Colin - Karen resolved to find more ways of responding positively to that group. She also reported that the activity had been helpful for her in giving her a recorded picture of her actions. The next step was to have her verbal and non-verbal behaviour match so that the pupils were not confused by having conflicting messages!

Of course observation schedules are useful for teachers to use alone in their classrooms too. They can record e.g. patterns of discussion with and without the teacher. Example 2 shows this.

Example 2. Topic: Discussion. Teacher: Tony

Tony tells of his experience

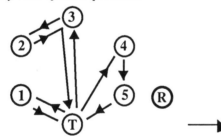

1. Gail
2. Harry
3. Joanne
4. Samantha
5. David
R. Recorder, Tom
T. Teacher
⟶ Direction of talk

Discussion Group A   Topic: Building houses on a wildlife preservation zone.

.

"I found that this observation schedule was useful at the evaluation stage of my research and in this case the pupils themselves made the observations and recordings. For my research I wanted to discover ways of getting the pupils to take more responsibility for their own learning. I had a new

class of Yr 2 pupils and they were strangely reluctant to do anything without my approving what they were doing. They wanted me to be involved first hand in the proceedings. How was I to begin....? Well, I thought I'd try having discussions in small groups to encourage all the youngsters to speak out and I went from group to group seeing if they were able to discuss. The trouble was that whenever I appeared the talking stopped and we had a teacher —>pupil—>teacher interaction just as if we had been in a formal classroom situation.

I explained to the pupils that they should speak amongst themselves as it were, and that they should involve everyone in the group in the discussion.....asking questions, begging explanations, even arguing if they felt the need. Most of all I wanted them to manage without me so that they could see that I was not essential to things happening.

After the children had several turns the interaction was more animated; certainly more things were being said, but unfortunately some children were dominating their group and others were still making no contribution. So I decided to try recording the pattern of the interaction. One pupil was recorder for each group and the task was to record the direction of the pupils' talk. The pupils seemed to enjoy this......they just had to talk you see, they didn't have to say anything significant....I was just measuring quantity, not quality, and so they were quite relaxed.

After a bit, the recording schedules became very messy and difficult to read but I think they got the discussions going, and after the pupils had made one or two comments they were less nervous about speaking out in public. Gradually they began to suggest topics and I became able to stay out of the interaction altogether. When I did this, I asked the groups to summarise the findings for the class and this gave them more practice, this was an extension of them 'speaking out'.

And so the pupils gained some confidence and generally speaking I was pretty pleased with the result. The schedules showed that discussion techniques were improving and that the pupils were managing better without me. That's what I'd been aiming for."

And so it can be seen that many kinds of investigations can be helped by using observation schedules. Sometimes at the start, drawing them up seems unnecessarily tedious but they do produce surprises. The main thing is that schedules produce objective evidence of carefully planned work rather than a series of impressionistic statements which cannot really be counted as research findings.

To ensure clarity in recording and later in reporting, the following information should appear on an observation schedule

1. The topic being observed.
2. The subject(s) (teacher, pupils(s)).
3. The number of subjects.
4. The number of observers.
5. Details of the coding used.
6. The timing schedule.

Once the schedule is drawn up it can be piloted by asking people to try it out. Then it becomes apparent if they have understood the coding and if the task is reasonable i.e. if it is realistic to ask observers to record the intended amount of detail. If amendments are required they can be made before the actual research study takes place. Then the recorder can concentrate on observing, rather than being distracted by an over-elaborate or over-simplistic recording system.

Observing and recording attitudes

Often teachers say that they wish to record their pupils' attitudes to their work (by observation techniques), especially if they are setting out to monitor any change in attitude over a period of time. They seem very reluctant to agree that this is a contentious move and that a safer way forward would be to record a change in behaviour patterns. Teachers often prevaricate on how these recordings would differ, taking refuge in comments like "I'd be a funny kind of teacher if I didn't know whether _____ was being lazy or not".

However, I would suggest that if you do wish to record

attitudes and/or attitude change through observation you make it clear that the recording is your interpretation and that you realise you may be mistaken! Provide evidence to substantiate any claims you *do* make. Omit claims like "John was bored stiff" and say something like "John appeared reluctant to be involved in the activity as he was very slow in coming to where the group was to work." You don't really know what John was thinking, he may have been nervous rather than bored, he may have preferred to do something else. It is fatally easy to make mistakes concerning attitudes - facial expressions and body postures can be very misleading. Take care!

5

Data analysis

Carrying out action-research is really a continuous process of analysis from start to finish. The first analysis begins when teachers reflect on their competencies and their classrooms and decide on a topic for study. The analysis will have involved them in asking "What, in this context would I like to improve?" and "How can I go about it?" And so *reflection/analysis* (i.e. looking back) and *interpretation* (i.e. looking forward) go hand in hand. The interpretation is guided by the teachers' experience and information gleaned from the literature on the topic, and leads into the formulation of the hypothesis, "If I do _____ then _____ is likely to occur", or the more open-ended research question e.g. "What strategies can I use to promote _____ ?"

Teachers would also wish to ascertain at this stage that the topic or problem was a fairly consistent feature of their teaching and not a one-off occurrence. Considering the frequency is important because only then can teacher-researchers be sure that they have selected a significant problem where improvement will have really important consequences.

If this initial analysis is difficult, if teachers know they have a problem but are not sure of its cause, then other means can be used to help. A colleague may be willing to observe and discern what is amiss, or video-recording a lesson may help, or pupil perceptions of what is happening could give very valuable and probably truthful feedback. These can be quite difficult strategies and are dependent on the social relationships which exist, but they should be considered. Pupils have been known to make sophisticated and helpful analyses and to do so in an adult manner. After all, they are the recipients of the teachers' performance. Videos, on the other hand can be re-played in private and even allowing for the effect on teaching behaviour, can indicate pointers for improvement. This process, i.e. involving other people or different media in observing and checking is known as triangulation.

Triangulation, i.e. the 'uncontaminated' perceptions of different people sharing their observations, can also very usefully feature during the evaluation phase of the action research. Comparing and contrasting and discussing perceptions of events can help the researchers to have reliable results. It is only too easy for researchers to see what they are looking for - especially when the hoped teaching change is some kind of improvement. Other people's perceptions of events are likely to keep one's feet firmly on the ground. Good research leads to deeper understanding of the *real* state of play which may be an explanation why things have *not* improved!

The final data analysis comes when all the information gathered is finally organised and the final claim(s) are to be made. These claims must reflect the number of people who were involved and the size of the action that was taken and so admit the limitations of the findings which emerged. Classroom action-research is usually akin to Case Study research when a great deal of information is gathered about a particular change which took place in one context. Although the teacher/researcher(s) and the pupils in this situation have reacted in certain ways and found out certain things, there can be no assurance that the same effect would occur with different people in different circumstances. And so no claim to generalisation should be made.

The same restriction holds for a questionnaire which has been answered by e.g. just one group of parents. There is no guarantee that other groups of parents in that school, far less other parents in other schools, would make the same kind of response. Action-researchers must not invalidate their work by making claims which clearly cannot apply. What they *can* do is report their research process accurately and in detail. In this way other teachers can understand the rigour and the discipline which structured the study. They can picture unfolding events. They can extract features of that situation and compare them to their own, making empathy (i.e. shared understanding) a more serious possibility.

▼▼▼Some action-research revisited...

In the light of all the new knowledge about action-research, let's look back now at one of the four pieces of research which was being talked about in Chapter 1.

Let's apply the principles of action-research to that study and evaluate it in terms of what the teacher-researcher did. You might like to use the check list to do this.

Check list			
	Yes	No	Comments
Data analysis (1) Identifying a problem			
Finding helpful literature			
Data analysis (2) Frequency of occurrence			
Refining a research question			
Planning an action on the basis of information			
Checking access			
Carrying out the action			
Taking care to reduce bias			
Triangulation			
Data analysis (3) Evaluation			
Generalisation			

Remember Jean, the learning support teacher who worked with Kevin(12)? Jean's research topic was chosen for her, as it were,

67

because Kevin's clumsiness and his deteriorating behaviour presented her with a real problem. Her first reflection on her current state of knowledge and understanding about clumsiness, or as she later termed the syndrome, motor impairment, caused her to realise that she could not without recourse to the specialist literature, diagnose Kevin's problem and she immediately found texts to help her do that. At the same time she observed Kevin in as many different environments as she could (school, playground, outside school) to gauge the extent of his disability, and in noting the frequency of the difficulty Jean could anticipate that any improvement in helping Kevin to move more effectively would be a worthwhile achievement. At this stage she began to formulate the hypothesis that if Kevin could complete all sorts of daily routine jobs more efficiently, his overall classroom behaviour would improve. Her initial plan was to test this hypothesis. However at this stage Jean did not know what was causing Kevin's problem or if and how she would be able to do anything to help and so she changed her approach, preferring the more open-ended research question(s), stage 1..... "Why is Kevin Clumsy?", and (after reading then carrying out the advised tests of motor impairment and as a result of diagnosing that balance was the underdeveloped skill), stage 2 ..... "Will activities specifically designed to help balance, help Kevin?"

To assist the diagnosis Jean invited the co-operation of the P.E. teacher who had specialist knowledge and much more experience in the observation of movement patterns. That teacher, and once the time-consuming nature of the remedial programme was known, other teachers became involved in carrying the programme through. They also acted as observers and evaluators, as they saw the effect of the programme and also Kevin's behaviour in other classes, away from the lunch time scene.

The research action consisted of carrying out the balance activity programme which was described in the literature. Several children were invited to join in and the activities were carried out at lunch times. Ostensibly the children were asked by the P.E. teacher to help her try out some ideas for her younger classes but they soon became interested in the scoring procedures and their improving scores...and the reason *why* they were participating became unimportant to them. The 'scores' provided concrete evidence of improvement in Kevin's balance in specific 'closed' skills. Jean recorded the other teachers' observations of more efficient movement in other more general classroom situations. In making her claims as to the outcomes of the research she was careful to acknowledge the other factors which could have influenced her results. These were the extra attention that Kevin had had and the other kinds of help e.g. the advice to approach tasks more slowly.

And so, while Jean was able to say with confidence that Kevin's balance had improved, she did not generalise or claim that this would happen for all the children who undertook this same programme (because they would have other degrees of impairment, other teachers and other kinds of responses). She did hope however, that after reading her research story any other teacher with a child like Kevin might be encouraged to try to find what was wrong and to try to improve the disability. At the end of her research Jean was pleased to say that she had found out why Kevin had a motor problem and that she had tried to do something to help. She claimed that she would be much more confident in identifying and tackling motor problems in the future. She hoped to make a study of observing movement patterns in much younger children and to find how early remediation could take place.

And so, one teacher's research idea had led to a collaborative venture. It had also stimulated the teacher to conceptualise other possible pieces of research in the motor impairment field. She considered that self appraisal→action-research → self development had been a natural sequence of events.

Action research, then is hard work needing a great deal of care at every stage. It is, however tremendously enriching and rewarding, giving to teachers as it does, a sure way of finding out why...!

6

Writing a research report

The Research Report is a record of the *process* of your action-research in school. The record is sub-divided into several chapters which sequentially house details of conceptualising and refining the research idea, then planning, implementing and evaluating the action. This format provides a structure for the research 'story'.

Although writing up happens in retrospect, these notes, read at the start can help you to make decisions about the scope and extent of your investigation for knowing what you have to report should help you plan what you have to do. Additionally they can help you organise your references, field notes, transcriptions and other materials into the appropriate sections and allow you to spread the writing load if this is what you would prefer to do.

Before considering the composition of the report it might be helpful to have a few reminders:

1. Think of your reader as an 'educated lay person' who has not been involved in any discussions about the work. This means that while you would explain terms like action-research because you could not assume a shared understanding of what this was, you could realistically expect that your reader would know and understand words such as curriculum or ability grouping or learning support. Explaining these would make the report cumbersome.

2. Write in the first person e.g. "I chose this. . ." or "My findings showed . . .". This preserves the individual character of your research and your report, it helps keep the text user-friendly and helps the reader to empathise with the unfolding events.

3. Keep the purpose of the research clearly in mind as you write. You are carefully planning an action which will enhance your teaching and through that the pupils' experience. You are then monitoring the effects of that action in such a way that you can

produce objective evidence of its effectiveness. In this way you can explain whether and in what ways the action has or has not helped you to improve your teaching and/or the pupil's learning.

4. In similar vein, remember that once you have formulated your research question or hypothesis you are gathering information to answer that question or to test that hypothesis. The reader should be able to link the question to the action to the findings and discern a clear sequence of events.

5. Use the past tense throughout the report (even although in Chapters 1 - 3 you are anticipating the action.)

6. There is not one absolute way to write the report. You may wish to alter this plan to suit your investigation. If so, look at other Research Reports for alternative strategies and discuss your plan with your tutor.

The format of the Report

Cover: *Title,* Name of Author, Name of Tutor

Pre-text: Acknowledgements
Index
Synopsis

Text   The Introduction
Chapter 1:   The Review of Literature
Chapter 2:   The Research Method
Chapter 3:   The Research Context
Chapter 4:   The Findings
Chapter 5:   Conclusions and Recommendations

Post-text   Bibliography

Appendices

Pre-Text

1. Acknowledgements

Here you should briefly offer thanks to those who have centrally contributed to the investigation and to the compilation of the final report, e.g. your tutor, the school personnel - teacher, pupils, and parents. In these cases abbreviate names, (e.g. Mrs. T, pupils L, A and B) to preserve anonymity. You would probably also wish to thank the librarian for helping with literature searches, and the typist for the presentation of the final report.

2. The Index

This should be clearly set out and accurate.

3. The Synopsis

The Synopsis is a *brief overview* of the entire process of the research. Write this last of all. Complete the text and then 'stand back' and ask "What are the critical points in each chapter? What is the essential information which will provide the reader with a skeleton framework of events?" Probably you would wish to explain the purpose of your research, the guidance you obtained from the literature, the research question or hypothesis which you formulated (as a result of reflecting, reading and contextualising), the action you took and the research strategy which guided your investigation. You would then say what you found out and what you considered would be the next logical step in any subsequent investigation.

The Text

1. The Introduction

In the introduction you are setting the scene for your reader. You could usefully share the thinking and reflection which caused you to select your particular topic; you would probably wish to explain the process of refining the original idea into a small-scale piece of action research and show how the literature helped you to formulate your research question or hypothesis. Thereafter you would very briefly describe the action you intended to take and finally say what teaching enhancement you hoped to gain as a result of carrying out this piece of action-research in the classroom. Some contextual information might be included here if it influenced e.g. the choice of topic, but there is a whole chapter later so consider carefully where this would best be placed.

2. *The Review of Literature*

In the review you are showing how your reading has informed your action. In what ways has the literature deepened your understanding? Have you found that other researchers have investigated your topic? What have they discovered? Have different authors produced conforming or conflicting evidence from their studies? Are you trying out any of their ideas in another context or are you developing their action plan in some way? What question/hypothesis emerges from your reading? Is this in line with your own reflection on your own experience or are you stimulated to test something which surprised you, but which, nonetheless you anticipated would be helpful for your teaching?

In Stage 1 of your survey of the literature you probably scanned many articles in journals, chapters in books, policy documents, etc. - in fact any reading which remotely concerned your topic. But as your topic and your action began to crystallise, you probably selected texts which dealt with the specific issue rather than the general topic. These are the ones which should feature most strongly in your review. The reader wants to know how the literature helped you to understand and to act, so try to be selective in what you read and what you report.

Use quotations and paraphrasing to emphasise the points you wish to make in your report but avoid 'quoting for the sake of it'. It is not helpful for the reader to have a series of quotations without explanation of why they have been chosen or even any indication of how they have extended your understanding or influenced your action.

The selection and study of a small number of key texts can show that you have been thinking critically about the action. These can stimulate argument and discussion which directly impinges upon your research question/hypothesis. This is much more useful than using many sources which are only marginally connected to the topic.

Be sure to check that all references are clearly and accurately recorded in the Bibliography. Avoid plagiarism at all costs.

74

3. The Research Method

In this chapter you state or re-state your research question or hypothesis i.e. you say what it is you are going to investigate. (You are likely to have written this at the end of your Review of Literature chapter but insert it again here so that the chapter has a sense of totality.) Then describe what action you are going to take to collect evidence to answer the question or test the hypothesis. In this chapter you reassure your reader that your action has been carefully planned according to the principles of action-research.

The application of these principles will vary according to the research strategies you select but you would want to show that they have been at the forefront of your planning. For example you would explain what you did to reduce bias in the collection of data (e.g. recording observations at different times of the day, involving the teacher as another observer to be able to compare findings, selecting a random sample of parents to complete questionnaires, using evidence from the children's work to endorse claims made, tape-recording interviews to gain accurate transcriptions).

You might also wish to justify your choice of strategy e.g.

"At first I considered distributing a questionnaire to allow me to find what a larger number of people thought, but on reflection I decided to hold just three interviews. As the issue '_____' was complex, the interview would allow the respondents to explain their responses. This would prevent the data degradation which occurs in using questionnaires".

This chapter also gives you the opportunity to demonstrate how carefully you planned your action e.g.

"I decided to hold the small group discussions in the Library corner. This was a quiet area with a plug for the tape-recorder and although there would be some background noise on the tape, the four children did not have to be taken out of the classroom - a move which could have caused them to think that something special was afoot and perhaps inhibited their contribution to the discussion. Staying in a familiar place was a calculated move to reduce bias in the collection of data."

This kind of account shows that you are taking cognisance of the principles of action-research, and that you are trying to collect evidence which is objective and reliable.

If you are using a Case Study approach or involving just a small number of people, you would discount any claims to generalisation at this point.

4. The Context

In this chapter you describe the people and the places and say what features caused you to choose a particular topic or to amend one. This amendment might happen pre-action or you might have to adapt to circumstances as they arise. Action research has the capacity to respond to this kind of change - and if this happens it would be very worthwhile for you to explain what occurred e.g.

> "*I had intended to concentrate on developing self-assessment in creative writing with four children in the top ability group. I wanted to find what criteria the children used to assess their own work. However, I found that while it was very difficult to get them to talk about their own work, they were very willing to discuss someone else's writing. So I changed my plan and began with peer-assessment. Only when this was established could I go back to self-assessment by asking the children 'Would these points apply to your own story?' This meant that three interactions went by before I could gather information on self-assessment. As I particularly wanted to find out about self-assessment, however, I did not alter my research question. I saw the first part as Stage 1.*"

Other researchers might have chosen to change the focus of the research to peer assessment. Then they would have had to describe the change and explain why it was made.

This chapter describing the context is very important in that it allows the readers to visualise and evaluate the action in context. It also helps them to compare and contrast features of the research situation to others within their own experience, making empathy more likely.

5. The Findings

The action has been taken and the important question(s) have been asked. The Findings chapter tells what was discovered. Remember that you are presenting evidence which will answer the research question or show whether the hypothesis was confirmed or denied.

It is sometimes difficult to decide what evidence should appear in the text and what should go into the appendices. The reader needs enough information in the text so that constant turning to the appendices is unnecessary. On the other hand the reading should not be constantly interrupted by figures and tables especially if they are not central to the understanding of the text. Try to achieve a balance of critical information in the text with illustrative information in the appendices.

Questionnaires

As a general rule, information from closed questions can be tabulated or represented in diagrammatic form within the text (see notes on data gathering procedures). This allows the reader to interpret the statistical evidence in the light of the explanation which follows. It is usual to display numbers as percentages - this also means that you must declare how many people formed the sample e.g. (N = 30). This gives the reader the scope of the survey and provides a more realistic interpretation of the figures. Diagrams should be helpful, not inserted just for variety. There is no need to produce a pie chart to show a 70 : 30 division.

It is more difficult to accurately represent the answers from open questions but these are interesting and important for your report. You would certainly take care to give a representative view of the returns perhaps quoting from parts of several transcriptions to give authenticity. You could also use 'unusual' replies but inform the reader that this is the case so that an as-accurate-as possible account of the evidence is transmitted. Then, insert one or two completed questionnaires in the appendix (probably one with an unusual reply if this has been quoted in the text). This allows the reader to judge the clarity of the questions and whether you have drawn legitimate inferences from the replies. Be sure to retain all of the completed questionnaires in case they are required later.

Interviews

It is important that the reader has access to the interview schedule and this should be placed in the appendix along with the transcriptions of the interview which provide information, interest and authenticity. While it may be unnecessary for you to transcribe complete interviews (you would need to check this), it is helpful if critical passages can be reproduced. Again actual quotations can appear in the text. As with the questionnaires, retain the tape-recordings as these may be required later.

Observation Schedules

Although these should mainly be in the appendix, extracts can usefully feature in the text. Perhaps these can provide immediate comparison between two events or show the difference in children's responses. Placing them in the text should illuminate the discussion not make it cumbersome, so again it is a question of using your judgement.

Examples of children's work

While these are always interesting, remember that they are only relevant if they provide evidence to answer the research question/hypothesis. Some examples can usefully provide evidence of e.g. changes over time or of increased motivation . . . but be sure you know why they have been included. They have to be informative not simply decorative!

6. Conclusions and Recommendations for further Research

The final chapter is an opportunity for you to reflect on your findings in the light of your action and to draw some conclusions e.g. in what ways have you gained insights or increased your understanding and how has this improved your teaching and/or the child's experience in the classroom? Were the strategies you used effective or given another chance would you have done different things? In what ways would you expect this to affect the outcome? What do you think you might do now to improve your teaching?

And finally, you might like to comment on whether action-research was a useful and realistic tool for you. Did it help you to reflect on and improve your teaching?

Post Text

1. Bibliography
In this section, provide all the information which a reader would require to find the original source - London as the place of publication can be omitted. All references included in the text must feature in the Bibliography.

Examples
Book
    Tizard, B. and Hughes, M. (1984) *Young children learning: Talking and thinking at home and at school.* Fontana

Chapter in Book
    Kemmis, S (1983). Action-research. In Husen, T. and Postlewaithe, T. (Eds), *International Encyclopedia of Education: Research and Studies.* Pergamon Press, Oxford.

Journal Article
    Dillon, J. (1983). Problem Solving and Findings. *The Journal of Creative Behaviour*, 30(2)

Policy Documents
    Department of Education and Science (1980). *A Framework for the School Curriculum.* HMSO.

These examples are based on guidelines from the Publication manual of the American Psychological Association. 3rd ed.

References within the Text
    In the text, reference to the author's name and year of publication is all that is required.

Example:
"While Smith (1988) claims that National Testing is a retrograde step, Jones (1989) endorses the move to test children at P4 and P7, and argues that the mechanism will raise standards".

2. Appendices
This section houses workcards, tables, graphs, examples of interview transcripts etc. i.e. all the instruments which were used to
collect data or to store/analyse it. These are placed at the back so
that they do not interrupt the main text.

N.B.
(Different educational institutions have their own requirements for
their research students. This format is the one followed at Moray
House for the B.Ed.(Hons.) Primary Course).

Bibliography

This bibliography is coded to allow easier identification of texts. The texts are some of those which the teachers and student teachers participating in the action-research project found particularly helpful.

1 Research
2 Early Education
3 Self-concept
4 Personal and Social Development
5 Learning Strategies and Study Skills
6 Child Development
7 Creativity
8 Problem-solving
9 Questioning and Discussion
10 Cooperative Learning
11 Bilingualism
12 Motor Impairment
13 Stress
14 Health Education

Bee, H. (1990) *The Developing Child* (5th edition) Harper & Row, New York   2,3,6

Bennett, N. and Cass, A. (1988) 'The effects of group composition on group interactive processes and pupil understanding', *British Education Research Journal,* 15, 19-32.   10

Bennett, N. and Dunne, E., (1989) *Implementing Cooperative Groupwork in Classrooms.* Paper presented at the conference of the European Association for Research in Learning and Instruction, Madrid.   10

Berman, L. (1970), *Towards New Programs for Young Children: Program and Research Possibilities.* College Pack. University of Maryland.   7

Blenkin, G. (1988) *Education and Development: Some implications for the Curriculum in the Early Years* . Harper & Row. 2,6

Brown, A., Brandsford, J. F., Cerrara, R. and Campione, J. (1983) 'Learning and Remembering and Understanding' in J. H. Flavell and E. M. Markman (eds) *Handbook of Child Psychology: Cognitive Development Vol. 2*   5

Brown, S., (1990) *Planning Small-Scale Research.* Scottish Council for Research in Education, Edinburgh   1

Burns, R. (1982) *Self Concept Development and Education.* Holt, Rinehart and Winston Ltd. East Sussex.   3,4

Chazan, M., Laing, A. and Harper, G. (1978) *Teaching Five to Eight Year Olds. Theory and Practice in Education.* Basil Blackwell.   6

Child, D. (1986) *Psychology and the Teacher* (4th Edition) Holt, Rinehart and Winston Ltd. East Sussex   3,4,5,7

de Corte, E. (1990) Towards powerful learning environments for the acquisition of problem-solving skills.' *European Journal of Psychology of Education,* 5-19   8

Dillon, J. (1983) Problem Solving and Findings. *The Journal of Creative Behaviour,* 30(2) .   9

Dillon, J. (1985) Using questions to foil discussion. *Teaching and Teacher Education,* 1.   9

Dunnett, J. D. (ed) (1986) *Diagnosis of and Possible Remedial Measures for Minimal Motor Impairment in School Children.* Moray House, Edinburgh.   12

Ebbutt, D. (1983) *Educational Action-Research: some general concerns and specific quibbles.* Cambridge Institute of Education, mimeo.   1

Fisher, R. (1990) *Teaching Children to Think*. Blackwell: Oxford.
5

Gow, L. and MacPherson, A. (1980) *Tell them from Me*. Aberdeen University Press.

Gurney, P. (1987) Self-esteem enhancement in Children: a review of research findings in *Educational Research*, Vol. 29 No. 2.
3

Hopkins, D. (1985) *A Teacher's Guide to Classroom Research*. Open University Press, Milton Keynes.
1

Hutt, C. (1979) 'Exploration and Play' in B. Sutton-Smith (ed) *Play and Learning*. Gardner Press.
2

Kemmis, S., (1983) 'Action-research' in Husen, and Postlethwaite, T. (eds) *International Encyclopedia of Education: Research and Studies*. Pergamon Press.
1

Lawrence, D. (1978) *Self-esteem in the Classroom*. Harper Row.
3,4

Lewis, I. & Munn, P. *So You Want to do Research? A guide for teachers on how to formulate research questions*. Scottish Council for Research in Education, Edinburgh.
1

McBeath, J. (1989) P.S.E. - What does it mean? in Kirk, G. and Glaister, R. (eds) *Professional Issues in Education*. Scottish Academic Press.
4

McCail, G. (1989) *The four year old in the classroom*. BAECE
2

Mitchell (1987) *Assessing the Language Skills of Bilingual Primary Pupils*. Scottish Council for Research in Education, Edinburgh
11

Mitchell (1987) *Implementing a Child-Centred Approach to Primary Schooling in a Bilingual Setting.* Scottish Council for Research in Education, Edinburgh.   11

Munn, P. & Drever, E. (1991) *Using Questionnaires in Small-Scale Research: a teacher's guide.* Scottish Council for Research in Education, Edinburgh.   1

Nisbet, J. and Shucksmith, J. (1984) T*he Seventh Sense: Reflections on Learning to Learn.* Scottish Council for Research in Education, Edinburgh.   5

Nisbet, J. and Shucksmith, J. (1986) *Learning Strategies.* Routledge Education Books.   5

Open University in Association with Pre-School Playgroups (1988) 'Playing together' in *The Pre-School Child.* Ward Lock Educational.   2

Rosenthal, T. and Zimmerman, B. (1978) *Social Learning and Cognition.* Academic Press.   5, 3, 4

Sinnott, E. W. (1970) 'The Creativeness of Life' in P. E. Vernon (ed) *Creativity.* Penguin Education.   7

Slavin, R. (1983) *Cooperative learning.* Longman.   9

Slavin, R. (1987) Developmental and motivational perspectives on co-operative learning: a reconciliation. *Child Development,* 58,   10

Stevenson (1989) *'Tom': Using Play-tutoring to Integrate a Difficult Child in a Nursery School.* Scottish Council for Research in Education, Edinburgh   2

Stott, Moyes and Henderson (1984) *Test of Motor Impairment.* Brook Educational Publishing, Guelph, Ontario   12

Tizard, B. and Hughes, M. (1984) *Young children learning: Talking and thinking at home and at school.* Fontana 2

Torbert, W. (1981) 'Why Educational Research has been so Uneducational' in P. Reason and J. Rowan (Eds) *Human Enquiry.* John Wiley. 1

Torrance, E. P. and Rockenstein, Z. L. (1970) 'Styles of Thinking and Creativity' in Ronald R. Schmuck (ed) *Learning Strategies and Learning Styles.* Plenum Press. 7

Wells, G. (1983) Talking with children: the complementary roles of parents and teachers. In M. Donaldson, R. Grieve and C. Pratt (eds) *Early Childhood Development and Education.* Blackwell: Oxford 2,6

Wood, D., Bruner, J. and Ross, G. (1976) The role of tutoring in problem solving. *Journal of Child Psychology and Psychiatry,* 17, 8

Publications

Special Educational Needs:
A Scottish Perspective

Series Editors: Gwynedd Lloyd and Judith Watson

Each volume in this acclaimed series:
* comprises a set of articles which focus on a particular theme
* brings together work and ideas across professional boundaries
* disseminates information and ideas to a wide
audience of interested professionals
* highlights the distinctive contribution of work within
the Scottish educational system

Volume 1
Innovatory Practice & Severe Learning Difficulties
Edited by Judith Watson

Volume 2
Chosen with Care? Responses to
disturbing and disruptive behaviour
Edited by Gwynedd Lloyd

Volume 3
Special Educational Needs Beyond 16
Edited by Alison Closs

Volume 4
A Curriculum for All?
5-14 and Special Needs
Edited by Elizabeth Jordan

Volume 5
Working with Communication Difficulties
Edited by Judith Watson

Volume 6
Gender and Special Educational Needs
Edited by Gwynedd Lloyd

Publications

Other titles from Moray House Publications

Vision for Doing
Assessing functional vision of learners who are multiply disabled
Stuart Aitken & Marianna Buultjens

Picture Books for Sharing
Forty picture books to talk about with young children
Alan Hill and Sheilah Jackson
(accompanying video available)

Bookmark
Edited by Jeffrey Aldridge
Articles on children's books; interviews with authors;
matters of concern and interest to all parents,
teachers, librarians and students

Pathfinder
Search-based problem-solving for learners
by Tom Conlon

Specific Learning Difficulties (Dyslexia)
A handbook for study and practice
Edited by Gavin Reid

Scottish Drama
A bi-annual journal for teachers of drama
Edited by Arthur Skelton

Publications

A full list of titles is available from:

The Publications Officer
Moray House Publications
Holyrood Road
Edinburgh EH8 8AQ
tel: 0131-558 6398
fax: 0131-558 3428